YOU ARE UNKILLABLE

Light Through The Dark Desert

Chidimma Doris Onuoha

Copyright © 2025 Chidimma Doris Onuoha

Editing & author services by Opulent Books: www.OpulentBooks.net

All Rights Reserved. No part of the book may be reproduced, stored in a retrieval system, or transmitted in any form or by any means, electronic, mechanical, photocopying, recording, or otherwise, without the prior written permission of the publisher. The only exception is brief quotations in book reviews.

Scriptures are taken from the New King James Version®. Copyright© 1982 by Thomas Nelson, Inc. Used by permission. All rights reserved.

First Printing, 2025

ISBN: 978-1-916691-15-5

TABLE OF CONTENTS

Dedication		1
Acknowledgements		3
Introduction		5
Chapter 1:	Learning to Obey God's Voice	9
Chapter 2:	Trying to Outrun God	25
Chapter 3:	Being Still	39
Chapter 4:	The Consequences of Disobedience	51
Chapter 5:	Desert Training	67
Chapter 6:	The Danger of Following the Crowd	111
Chapter 7:	The Blossoming of Destiny in the Desert	127
Chapter 8:	God of Second Chance	147
Chapter 9:	Answering When God Calls	167

Chapter 10:	God's Unconditional Love	185
Chapter 11:	Discomfort of the Chosen	199
Chapter 12:	Shedding Weights in the Wilderness	211
Chapter 13:	Dreams and Revelations	225
Chapter 14:	Being a Vessel	245
About the Author		261

DEDICATION

To my dear Mum,

You are no longer here, yet your memory lingers. I now comprehend the magnitude of your presence, only truly grasped in the echoing silence of your absence.

You were a rock, unbeknown to me. But then, we so often overlook the steadfast constants in our lives, the dependable rhythm beating gently in the background, until one day it halts.

You stood as a beacon of truth, illuminating our path, your wisdom unfolding like the petals of a flower beneath the sun. Your words were whispers in the wind, often ignored in our youthful rebellion, yet somehow, they found their way, taking root in the fertile soil of our hearts. Now, they bloom, a testament to your enduring influence.

You were unshakeable, unmoved by the tremors of life's adversities, your resilience echoing in the rhythm of our lives. You taught us integrity, the merit of walking the challenging path, the right path. Your voice, steadfast and certain, guided us through the maze of life.

And so, this book is dedicated to you, Mum. In honour of your unwavering truth, your resilience, and the love that continues to guide us. Your memory is etched into every page, a silent testimony to the woman whose strength forms the bedrock of my journey.

ACKNOWLEDGEMENTS

First and foremost, I would like to express my deepest gratitude to God, the author and finisher of our faith. Without His grace and guidance, this book would not exist. Your divine fingerprints are on every page, and I am immensely grateful for the journey you have led me on, which has brought this book into existence.

I extend my heartfelt thanks to Pastor Gideon. Your wisdom and compassion have been a beacon during my darkest moments. You have not just been a pastor but also a confidant, guide, and true spiritual father. Your persistence in helping me navigate through my bitterness, your ceaseless prayers, and your tireless efforts to help me find the path to forgiveness have been transformative. I will forever cherish the lessons learnt under your nurturing guidance.

I also want to extend my heartfelt gratitude to two special individuals who have played a significant role in my life:

Brother Nicholas Igbokwe, my prayer group leader in Nigeria. The man to whom God spoke, saying, 'Chidimma will not die, but I will allow them to torture her flesh.' He is a true man of God, and his unwavering support and divine insight have been a source of strength and inspiration throughout this journey.

Mrs Ugochi Obioha, a sister like no other. Despite my being older than her, I have found her shoulders wide enough for me to lean on each time the devil strikes. She has been my prayer partner and confidante during times of tears, the one who truly understands my dreams. She sees in me what others don't see, and her presence in my life has been a true blessing.

Lastly, I would like to express my sincere appreciation to my publisher, Joe Benjamin, and his dedicated team. You have expertly guided this book from a concept to a reality, and for that, I am deeply thankful. A special thank you to Ozioma Paul for your final contributions that added value to my story.

To all those named and unnamed who have journeyed with me, your impact is permanently imprinted within these pages. Thank you.

INTRODUCTION

You hold in your hands a story, but it is not merely my story, nor is it a mere retelling of life events. This book is a torch meant to guide you through the darkest nights, a beacon to remind you that you are not alone, and proof that there is a divine hand ready to lead you if you only dare to reach out. If you've ever felt lost or abandoned or that life has simply dealt you too many blows to keep standing, then this book is for you.

You Are Unkillable is not a title chosen lightly. Like Moses in the Bible, I found myself pursued from a tender age. Not by a Pharaoh, but by the tribulations and challenges that life had in store for me. The burdens of my family and those around me became mine, my life filled with confusion, hatred, sadness, and bitterness. This journey is filled with highs and lows, triumphs and trials, in a way I never expected when I first felt compelled to pen my story.

Moses was pursued from birth because he was a liberator, a leader, and a light. In my life, I have been pursued not for what I was but for what I could become—a ray of hope, a witness to resilience, a survivor. As you walk the chapters of this book, you will journey with me through despair and hope, rejection and acceptance, bitterness and forgiveness.

The motivation to write this book is rooted in my desire to inspire you, the reader, to understand that no matter how daunting your circumstances, you possess an innate strength that can guide you through. Life has a way of handing us the bitter fruits of experience, yet it is in the testing that we learn, grow, and find the resolve to keep moving forward.

In sharing my story, I hope to reveal to you that there is a deeper meaning to every experience we endure. I want to reassure you that abandonment by the world doesn't equate to abandonment by God. Sometimes, it's through our isolation that God calls us closer, whispering to us amidst the storm, 'I want to walk with you alone.'

Rejection, abandonment, betrayal—these experiences, as harsh as they may be, might simply be God's way of getting our attention. They may be painful lessons, but they are lessons, nonetheless. Remember, the night is darkest before the dawn, and it's

Introduction

in these moments of intense darkness that we can see the stars.

In writing this book, I hope to inspire you to trust God more, to understand that you are bigger and stronger than your circumstances, and to recognise that the voice of fear is often the smaller part of us that needs reassurance. Through this journey, you will come to understand that there's a bigger you, a version of yourself that is resilient, that is brave, that can withstand and overcome. This is the you that the Holy Spirit is cheering on, saying, 'You can do this! You've got this!'

Sometimes, we need to come down from the mountain tops of our pride, success, and self-reliance to truly listen to the voice of God. Growth often occurs not on the peaks of triumph but in the valleys of trials. Just like a plant needs both sunshine and rain to grow, we need experiences of joy and sorrow to fully mature.

So, as you turn these pages, open your heart to the possibility that you, too, can overcome adversity. You are capable of forgiveness, even in the face of deep-seated bitterness. You are not defined by how others treat you, but by how you respond and rise above it. Embrace the journey and remember that you are not alone. This is not just a story of survival, but a testament to the power of faith, resilience, and unyielding hope.

It is my hope that by the time you close the last page, you will have found strength, inspiration, and, most importantly, the reassurance that no matter what, God will always be there for you. There is always hope. There is always, always a way through.

Chapter 1
Learning to Obey God's Voice

On the 3rd day of October, under the bright sun, a declaration from the heavens reached Earth: 'Rejoice, for today a gift is bestowed upon you. It will be a girl, and she will be called Chidimma.' Which means God is good.

That's how my journey began in Imo State—Eastern part of beautiful Nigeria. I came into the world through my mother, Ulumma, a woman of extraordinary beauty and strength. From the moment I took my first breath, I was designated to be something more, a light, for my family and my generation.

The Earth celebrated as I arrived. The heavens themselves opened their windows, showering blessings down on the world below. I was an innocent yet fierce lioness, ready to take on the world that awaited me.

As a child, I grew up just like my peers. But there was something about me that set me apart. I was fearless, always standing for what was right. My intelligence was beyond my age, and my love for God was evident. I led praise and worship in my Block Rosary and local church. My voice, so melodious, could bring down angels from heaven. I wasn't ordinary. I was marked from childhood.

In my primary school days, I was outstanding. At the age of eight, I took part in inter-school drama competitions, playing the character of Adolphus Hitler in the drama titled *The Trial of Adolphus Hitler*. The role was so well executed that it earned me the nickname 'Adolph Hitler.' It was this role that brought me before governors of states, adding another dimension to my life that few could comprehend.

However, my success was a threat to others. The recognition I received attracted envy, especially from my male peers. I faced challenges and was beaten a couple of times out of jealousy.

Despite the struggles, I remained steadfast, my spirit never faltering. I stood tall, reminding myself of the declaration made at my birth—I was not ordinary; I was destined for greatness. My journey was only beginning, and I was ready to face whatever lay ahead.

From my childhood, I sensed an undeniable correlation between my life and that of a significant biblical figure, Moses. Just like Moses, whom God chose to lead the Israelites out of Egypt, I, too, felt a calling from an early age to be a beacon of light and a voice for my people.

In the Bible, Exodus 19:5 reads, 'Now therefore, if you will indeed obey My voice and keep My covenant, then you shall be a special treasure to Me above all people; for all the earth is Mine.' This was the command God gave to Moses for His people, a promise of protection and blessing hinged on obedience.

The path of obedience is not a smooth highway; it is a winding road filled with bumps, turns, and sometimes detours. It's human nature to question and to doubt, especially when the way forward is not clear. But in this chapter of my life, I was about to learn that even though the road was tough, the destination that God had in store for me was worth every struggle.

Just as Moses eventually learnt to listen to God and follow His guidance, I, too, would come to understand the power of trust and obedience in my journey. However, getting there would require a deep inner transformation—a journey of faith, resilience, and unyielding determination. This was the beginning of my journey, a path that would lead me from being a girl named Chidimma, born on a beautiful sunny day, to becoming the light of my generation.

My journey has taught me not to outrun God. I had to understand the true meaning of obedience. This was the foundation upon which my journey was built, the lesson that would guide me as I traversed the intricate maze of life.

Guarded by Destiny

At the age of ten, while I was in a school that trained future reverend sisters, I experienced a chilling ordeal. One day, overwhelmed with homesickness, I requested an exit card from the sister principal to go home. To my surprise, she granted my wish. I was ecstatic, but little did she know my home was a good four to five hours away. At such a tender age, embarking on such a journey alone was a dangerous proposition.

As I made my way, I reached a major stop after three and a half hours. Here, I naively boarded a taxi with two men inside. They seemed friendly enough and even offered me food and drink, which I gratefully accepted. Unbeknownst to me, the drink might have been laced with something intended to put me to sleep. But sleep eluded me. The men became increasingly agitated with each passing hour, making calls and discussing my unusual alertness.

As time passed, one of them had a change of heart. He emphatically told his partner that he wouldn't be a part of whatever they had planned for me. In the end, out of what seemed like fear and respect, they returned my money and safely placed me on a bus back home.

Upon arriving home, my family was taken aback. My father's first reaction was to question if I was a ghost or a human. It wasn't until recently that I fully comprehended the gravity of that event. It appears that from a young age, God had a bigger plan for me, one that sinister intentions wouldn't derail.

At the tender age of fourteen, I experienced a harrowing episode at school. I was stricken with a sudden and violent illness. My fellow students, gripped by concern, swiftly carried me to the principal's office. Recognising the gravity of my condition, the school authorities wasted no time rushing me to the hospital.

The following day, I underwent an emergency appendectomy. In the midst of this turmoil, the hospital staff reached out to my parents, who immediately came to my bedside. It was a moment of deep vulnerability and fear, yet their presence brought me comfort.

In the haze of my unconscious state prior to the surgery, I remember speaking to my mother about a distressing premonition involving a woman who harboured ill will toward me. I warned my mother in my delirium, pleading with her to beware of this relative who wished us harm.

This unnerving experience and my subsequent recovery have only deepened my faith in the healing and protective powers of God. It's a gentle reminder that even in our darkest hours, there is a greater light watching over us.

Pronounced Dead at Sixteen

The defining moment of my journey began when I was just 16 years old. Though I was young and inexperienced, I was a bright, intelligent child who felt a deep passion for Christ. However, the worldly temptations constantly pulled at my spirit, creating a tug-of-war between my faith and my desires. This spiritual struggle led me to aspire to become a reverend sister, but life had other plans.

Tragedy struck when, at the age of sixteen, I was pronounced dead. The world around me faded, and the grip of the unknown tightened. But as destiny would have it, my story wasn't over. Miraculously, I awoke surrounded by the sterile white walls of a hospital room. It was there, in that room, that inspiration struck, and I penned down my first song—a song that flowed from my heart, capturing the essence of my experience in my native dialect.

Though confined within the hospital's walls, I felt a newfound purpose. With a song in my heart and a fervour to inspire, I moved around the wards, serenading and praying for the other patients. Even in my weakened state, I became a beacon of hope for many.

The mystery of my ailment remained unsolved. Doctors couldn't pinpoint a cause, and all their tests came back inconclusive. Yet, inexplicably, I would oscillate between life and death, feeling the cold grip of the beyond, only to be brought back into the warmth of life.

I spent three arduous months in the hospital, but it was during this time that I believe my true ministry began. Looking back, I realise that this ordeal, as harrowing as it was, shaped my destiny and gave me a unique testimony that would inspire countless others. God kept me alive for a purpose, and I had not fully accepted God's call over my life.

The Crucial Voice of Obedience

God's voice is not like any other. It carries a certain weight, a divine essence, if you will. Listening to it can profoundly shape our journey in this world, often shortening our path through trials and tribulations. Yet, hearing that voice is one thing; obeying it is an entirely different matter.

Nearly two decades ago, I set out on my career path, full of youthful vigour and high hopes. Looking back now, I have nothing tangible to show for it. If only I had paid attention to what God was trying to tell me at the time, my story would have been different. Instead of being here, I might have been somewhere else, pastoring a church, coaching people, or doing God's work in another capacity. But alas, I kept pushing my agenda, ignoring the divine guidance that was so desperately trying to reach me.

God is patient, yes, but He respects our free will. When I stubbornly decided to take my journey into my own hands, God stepped aside. He watched, I imagine with a heavy heart, as the devil created havoc in my life. This was not out of a lack of care from God; rather, it was a consequence of my unwillingness to listen, to truly hear and obey His voice.

There were many times when His message was crystal clear. Amidst the daily grind, in moments of silence, even in my dreams, He tried to reach me. I dreamt of speaking to congregations, of winning souls for the kingdom. Yet, those visions fell on deaf ears. I didn't want to leave the comfort of my corporate bubble. The allure of worldly gains was too strong, the notion of a spiritual mission too intimidating.

I chose to run away from the calling, and in doing so, I was trying to outrun God. But the thing about trying to outrun God is that He is always there, waiting for us to tire from our futile race, ready to embrace us when we finally stop running.

Looking back, I now understand the importance of obeying God's voice. He was trying to steer me away from unnecessary heartache, to save me from wandering aimlessly in a wilderness of my own making.

This is not just my story; it's a lesson for all who are willing to listen. Obedience to God's voice isn't just about following rules; it's about aligning ourselves with a divine plan that promises a life full of purpose and fulfilment. So, let's not be like the earlier version of me, the one who refused to listen. Instead, let's walk in obedience, for it is the key that unlocks the door to our divine destiny.

The Unanswered Call

As I delve deeper into my story, it's crucial to note that my life wasn't solely marred by disobedience. I faced an array of trials and tribulations that, in hindsight, were masterfully orchestrated by the devil himself. He had a vested interest in derailing me from my divine calling, an endeavour I'll explore in later chapters.

Growing up, my life was rooted in the church, thanks largely to my parents, particularly my mother. From the tender age of seven, I became a participant in the Catholic church's Block Rosary. Each Christmas season, we'd go from house to house, carolling and spreading the Word of God. My passion for the Lord led me to a Catholic secondary school, Daughters of Divine Love Juniorate, forsaking the institution where my elder sister was studying. I had dreams of becoming a reverend sister.

God painted vivid pictures in my dreams of me serving His people, speaking and winning souls over to Him. Yet, even with this clarity, my heart was set on a different path. My voice wasn't merely for singing; it was an instrument of ministry. Not because of its beauty, but due to the potent anointing it carried. The only true fulfilment I felt was when I stood before an audience, microphone in hand, ministering through song.

At the age of twenty-two, I released my first album, *Sufficient Grace*. It received wide acclaim, with the largest TV stations broadcasting it, and I'd often receive calls from people who'd seen me perform on television. Yet it wasn't about my voice per se, but the anointing it carried. There were moments when I'd start to sing, and people would be moved to tears, falling under the weight of the anointing. What is more spectacular about this song is the circumstances around when I received it and how it pointed me to a greater purpose, even though I was unaware of it then. I had just joined a state government house in Nigeria as a national corps member, where I served for a year. Sometime during my service, I found favour with my boss and was offered a barge to manage. This was a huge deal because the barge was to be used for transporting oil produce, and it would be the start of my journey as a millionaire. However, unfortunately, on the first trip to receive the barge, I got news that the barge sank! It was beyond devastating because I genuinely hoped this would be the big break that would set me up for success in life. Now, in retrospect, I see how that worked together for me because if I had been down that path of transporting oil produce, I might have been even further separated from the divine call upon my life.

Despite these clear signs of a divine calling, my heart was set on securing a white-collar job. God would nudge me, urging me to follow His path, but I stubbornly resisted. I vividly remember my discomfort in several jobs I took. The environment was hostile; my colleagues were unwelcoming. Yet I remained, ignoring God's gentle promptings.

In Matthew 7:24, Jesus speaks about those who hear His words and act on them: 'Therefore whosoever heareth these sayings of mine, and doeth them, I will liken him unto a wise man, which built his house upon a rock.' But I was building my life on sinking sands, not the firm foundation of God's Word. I was hearing God's voice but not acting on His instructions.

Reflecting on this period of my life, I now realise that my disobedience was not a mere act of defiance. It was me relinquishing control of my life to external influences, succumbing to the devil's manipulations, and, most tragically, missing out on the fulfilment that comes with heeding God's voice.

Despite my defiance, my stubbornness, and my choice to walk my own path, one thing remained constant: God's hand was still on my life. His call, which was as insistent as the dawn, didn't diminish or waver. It was like a gentle whisper during a storm, a persistent echo in the chaos of my life, reminding me I was chosen, set apart for a purpose far greater than what I had in mind.

Even when I was lost in the world, seeking fulfilment in the wrong places, God never withdrew His calling. In His divine wisdom and boundless mercy, He waited. He waited for the prodigal daughter to return, waited for me to realise that the echoes of my divine purpose could not be drowned by worldly pursuits. And despite everything, His call endured, His hand remained, patiently guiding me back to the path I was born to tread.

This is the beautiful and enduring grace of our God—even when we fall, even when we lose our way, His love, His calling, and His hand never leave us. I am a testament to His unwavering faithfulness, and my story is a journey back to Him. The road has been rough, filled with detours and wrong turns, but it's a road that ultimately leads me back into the loving embrace of God and the destiny He has prepared for me.

Hearing God's Voice

God's voice, in my experience, isn't loud or demanding. He speaks softly, gently, and in a way that is calm. Often, our own thoughts can be loud and full of noise. These thoughts can seem like they're shouting at us, telling us what to do. But God doesn't shout. He speaks once, quietly and calmly. He isn't pushy or bossy.

I'm a person who has a lot of thoughts. Sometimes, my mind can be so full of ideas and worries that it's hard to hear anything else. But I've learnt how God talks to me. He often talks to me in dreams. When I have a dream, I know it's important. If I don't listen to these dreams and do something different, things rarely go well.

Even when things were tough, when I was going through chemotherapy and losing my hair, God spoke to me in a dream. I felt terrible about myself, but God told me that I couldn't be beaten. As I lay weak on a couch in the sitting room, I felt His presence. I saw Him come into the room, and He said to me, calling me by my name, **'You are unkillable'**. I don't know if that's the right English, but it's what He said. Since that day, I've held on to that dream. When things are hard, I remember that God told me I'm unkillable. No matter what the devil tries to tell me, I remember God's words.

So, how do you hear God's voice among your own thoughts and ideas? How do you tell the difference? In the next section, I will give some advice on how to listen to God more clearly. Let's remember Deuteronomy 28:1-14. I recommend that you read it in its entirety.

The scripture emphasises the importance of not only hearing but also obeying God's voice. This obedience brings about blessings that are all-encompassing, impacting every aspect of our lives. For me, this meant understanding that God's voice often comes softly, subtly, and through dreams. It means turning down the volume of my own thoughts and worries and focusing on the still, quiet voice of God. And, most importantly, it means having the courage to follow His guidance, even when it seems difficult.

Tuning in to God's Voice

Hearing God's voice can be a struggle, and I won't sugar-coat it. It's not an easy task because our minds are often a battlefield filled with various thoughts, ideas, and distractions. I, too, grapple with this, and I consider myself a work in progress in this regard.

So, what can you do? Firstly, clear the clutter in your mind. There are times, even as recently as a few days ago, when I've had to vocally command the storm of thoughts in my mind to be still. I've had to say, 'Evil thoughts, let me be. Holy Spirit, please take over.' The devil can run rampant in our minds, feeding us with negative and confusing thoughts. It's a struggle, but we can rebuke these voices and clear the mental clutter.

Secondly, stay away from toxic people and avoid unnecessary noise. They can cloud your thoughts and hinder you from hearing God's voice. What you listen to during the day often echoes in your mind when you're trying to connect with God. So, it's essential to limit these auditory distractions as much as possible.

Thirdly, seek solitude and quiet moments with God. It might be difficult, but even spending an hour in quiet contemplation can make a significant difference. During this time, you can read books that enrich your spirit and help you connect better with God's voice.

Fourthly, surround yourself with the right people. Their influence can guide your thoughts and actions towards a more spiritual path. A spiritual mentor or director can also be beneficial.

Having someone to listen to and gain wisdom from can help you discern God's voice better in your life.

This journey of hearing God's voice isn't easy, but with determination, the right environment, and proper guidance, it's achievable. The struggle may be real, but so are the rewards of connecting with God on a deeper level.

AFFIRMATIONS:

1. I diligently obey the Lord my God.
2. I'm watchful to do all the commandments which He commands me this day, and the Lord my God sets me high above all the nations of the earth.
3. I set my mind on God, and I tune out distractions through the help of the Holy Spirit.

Chapter 2

Trying to Outrun God

I often found myself drawn to the story of Jonah. You know the one—Jonah 1:1-17. It's a narrative of divine will against human reluctance, where God beckons Jonah to Nineveh, but he resists. Ultimately, in his attempt to flee, he's swallowed by a whale. A whale God had directed his way. This story, more than any other, resonated with me profoundly.

There's a particular incident I haven't shared with many, but it bears a remarkable semblance to Jonah's story. It was a day like any other. As I arrived at the office, the morning sun painted golden streaks on the high-rise buildings. The familiar scent of brewing coffee greeted me. But that day was going to be anything but ordinary.

Emmanuel, or 'Next Door' as I fondly called him due to our adjacent office spaces, was already at his desk. Our daily conversations had become a cherished routine. I'd walk into his office, sometimes weary from the weight of the world, and he'd jest, 'Next Door, you look like you haven't caught a wink! What's the matter? Too much telly or another one of your late-night philosophical ponderings?'

But that day, my entrance was different. Without introduction, I declared, 'Next Door, I am the Jonah in this situation.'

His eyebrows arched in surprise. 'What do you mean?'

At that time, I was in a difficult phase with my company. Being on a contract, the terms of my employment were often under scrutiny. Our union was locked in a battle, fighting for better wages and improved conditions. The pressure was tangible. Yet, amidst this chaos, I felt a divine unrest. A conviction that I was in the wrong place.

'That night,' I continued, 'I wrestled with God. I felt this overpowering sensation that I didn't belong in that setting. He had a different plan for me.'

Emmanuel leaned back, absorbing my words. 'So, you felt God calling you elsewhere, but like Jonah, you're resisting?'

I sighed. 'I adore God, truly. But there's this part of me that craves recognition, that wants things on my terms. I love Him, yet I'm torn between His will and mine.'

He nodded thoughtfully. 'It's a challenge, aligning our desires with His. But remember, just as Jonah couldn't outrun God's will, neither can we.'

Our chat lingered in my mind. Was I trying to escape my Nineveh? Running away from where God intended me to be? In my pursuit of personal glory, was I missing a divine calling?

For many of us, the struggle is real. We're torn between worldly desires and divine direction. But like Jonah, we must learn that we cannot outrun God's plan for us. Instead, we should embrace it, even if it leads us through the wilderness, for there will always be *'light through the dark desert'*.

What Is Trying to Outrun God?

The appeal of the fast lane attracted me. It wasn't just about the speed, but the stature it promised. I yearned to rub shoulders with the high-class ladies, to be seen, to be acknowledged. The world had set a benchmark for success, and I was desperate to not only reach it but to surpass it. I dreamt of being the best cost engineer, the epitome of excellence. And, in many ways, I achieved that. The awards on my mantlepiece bore testimony to my dedication and skill.

Yet, amidst the blinding spotlight and roaring applause, a voice deep within whispered that there was more. It wasn't a voice of discontentment; it was one of divine direction. I felt God urging me to slow down. Not because He wanted to halt my progress, but because He wanted to redirect it. He sought not to diminish my dreams but to refine them, aligning them with a grander design He had in mind.

But my internal compass was conflicted. While my soul was deeply anchored in God's love, my ambitions steered me toward the world's definition of success. I was running, sprinting even, towards what I believed was my destiny. Yet, the irony wasn't lost on me. For all my hurry, for all my aspirations, I found myself not moving forward, but rather lagging behind. Those I had once deemed competitors, peers in the race of life, now seemed miles ahead.

This brought me to a profound revelation. In my earnest attempt to outpace the world, I was inadvertently trying to outrun God. But what does it mean to try to outrun God? It is to chase after our own desires, even if they lead us away from His plans. It's the belief that our vision for our lives is superior to the one He's crafted. And the more we run, the more we find ourselves out of sync with His rhythm.

God's path isn't always about the speed or the accolades. It's about purpose, alignment, and growth. When we try to outrun Him, we aren't just defying a divine plan; we're missing out on the profound lessons, blessings, and experiences He has lined up for us. For in the quiet moments, away from the hustle, God imparts wisdom, strength, and a deeper understanding of our purpose.

In the end, the race isn't about who reaches the finish line first, but about who runs it with purpose, understanding, and divine alignment.

Ecclesiastes 9:11 says, 'I returned and saw under the sun that, The race is not to the swift, Nor the battle to the strong, Nor bread to the wise, Nor riches to men of understanding, Nor favor to men of skill; But time and chance happen to them all.' The true victory lies not in outpacing others, but in walking hand in hand with God, even if that means taking the longer, winding path through the dark desert, for His light will always guide the way.

The Cost of the Worldly Race

The quiet reflections of the past are often interrupted by piercing questions about the present. How did I feel, realising that my attempts to outrun God were doing more harm than good? It's a profound question and one I had to deeply introspect upon.

Spiritually, the race away from God left me malnourished. Even after years of knowing Him, I felt like a baby Christian, still learning to take my first steps. Many of my peers with whom I started this spiritual journey have since soared to great heights. Some have taken on pastoral roles, guiding others with wisdom and insight. Yet, here I was, still grappling with the basics. My hurried pace meant that I often overlooked the nourishment of God's Word, and I found it challenging to sit still and immerse myself in scripture.

Mentally and emotionally, this race took its toll too. The pressure to succeed, to constantly be on the move, weighed heavily on me. I remember the time after my tertiary education in Nigeria when we were required to serve our country for a year. It was an opportunity to contribute, to learn, and to grow. But even then, my focus was twisted. I sought postings that promised prestige and prosperity, even if it meant pulling some strings. I found myself in plush assignments, like the Government House, while many of my peers were dispatched to remote villages.

I recall the stark contrasts of those times. There I was, a young graduate with access to the corridors of power, while others of my age faced challenges in rural areas, some without even access to clean water. My position allowed me to be generous. I shared my resources, helping out those in need. But looking back, I realise that while they were building resilience, character, and a genuine understanding of life, I was blinded by the glitter of transient success.

Materially, I might have seemed prosperous. My ambitions were clear: make money, gain recognition, and ensure my family's well-being. Coming from a modest background, the drive to provide was strong. But in this relentless pursuit, I overlooked God's nudges. He wanted me to slow down, to perhaps further my education, to invest in personal growth. But my dreams were tinted with the hues of worldly success. I dreamt of flashy cars and a life of luxury, sometimes even against the wishes of my loved ones.

Now, as I stand at this juncture of life, I see the repercussions of those choices. The race to outrun God, to dictate my own path, has left me with profound lessons. It has taught me about the fragility of worldly success and the enduring nature of spiritual growth. The real race is not about outrunning God but about aligning oneself with His divine plan, understanding that His pace is intentional, filled with lessons, growth, and purpose. It's a lesson I hope others can glean from my journey, ensuring they don't make the same missteps in their own races.

Ignoring Divine Warnings Before Marriage

The embarrassing saga of my five-month marriage stands as a reminder of the havoc that ensues when we try to outrun God. Marriage is a sacred union, a commitment for a lifetime. Yet, in my haste and societal pressure, I ignored the unmistakable signs from the Lord.

I met a man, and God's voice was clear as day: 'This is not the one.' Yet, the ticking time clock and the societal expectations, especially in the African culture, blinded me. I felt the urge to 'move forward' with my life.

My desperation to find a husband clouded my judgement. I vividly remember the day I sat down with my pastor, presenting him with a list of three potential guys seeking divine guidance. He immediately pointed out the very man I eventually married, warning, 'Definitely not this person.' Yet, in a twisted turn of events, this man became my guy.

Despite multiple red flags, including a distressing incident at a hotel, I pressed on. I was more smitten by his mother's affection for me than the man himself. On reflection, every step leading to that ill-fated union was marred by signs I chose to ignore. Even my wedding attire wasn't spared, as the place it was stored in caught fire.

The absence of peace was evident. The Holy Spirit speaks to us in hushed tones, bringing calm and clarity. In contrast, the devil is loud, persistent, and chaotic. From the very beginning, the union was shrouded in darkness and turmoil. I felt it—the lack of peace, the constant unrest. The Holy Spirit's voice was clear, but I chose the clamour of societal expectations over His gentle whisper.

One crucial lesson I learnt from this ordeal was the significance of peace. True peace—the kind that comes from aligning with God's will—acts as a compass, guiding us toward the right path. When we stray, the absence of this peace serves as a warning. Much like Jonah's story, where the turbulent seas signified his defiance of God's command, my life's storms were a testament to my disobedience.

In retrospect, I can see that every time I tried to speed ahead, God was asking me to pause, reflect, and align with Him. The race isn't about speed; it's about direction. And the right direction is always towards God.

Holding on to God's Hand When Things Go Bad

Life is a roller coaster of experiences—some joyous, others traumatic. There are moments when faith falters, and everything seems to crumble around you. But in those times, one thing has been clear to me: God's presence.

There were moments of sheer despair when the weight of the world threatened to crush me. But even in those darkest hours, I never entirely abandoned my faith. Some internal compass, perhaps God's gentle whisper, reminded me of His enduring love.

My life has been punctuated by near-death experiences. Ten surgeries, each more daunting than the last. Every time I found myself on the operating table, the odds seemed stacked against me. Yet, each time, I emerged as a witness to God's grace and protection. Many questioned, 'Why always surgery? Why not divine healing?' And while I didn't have all the answers, I knew that in every challenge, God was moulding and refining me.

On one occasion, after a particularly harrowing health scare, my company doctor, a seasoned professional of forty years, was left astounded. Reading my medical reports, he declared my survival 'medically impossible.' Yet, here I was, living proof of the miraculous. His words brought to mind others who weren't as fortunate as other individuals. Despite the grim outlook, I knew God had a purpose for me.

Interestingly, God often communicated with me through dreams, revealing glimpses of challenges ahead. These prophetic insights were my early warning system. Whenever I heeded these dreams and prayed about them, I was shielded from the impending troubles.

My life's journey, filled with pain and challenges, has been a testament to God's persistent presence. He's been my guiding light, even when I tried to outrun Him or doubted His plans. This unwavering faith isn't about ignoring life's hardships or pretending they don't exist. It's about recognising God's hand in every situation and believing He has a purpose for every trial. Just like Jonah, even in the midst of tumultuous waters, God is right there, guiding us back to His path.

Here are five practical things you can do to surrender to God's timing and pace:

1. **Patience:** Surrendering to God's timing is a journey. You can't expect instant transformation, but with patience, understanding, and perseverance, you'll gradually align with God's divine plan (James 1:4).

2. **Understand the Devil's Tactics:** Be aware that the devil knows your weaknesses and will consistently try to divert you from your path. Recognising these tactics is the first step towards countering them (1 Peter 5:8).

3. **Seek God's Voice:** Identify that unique place or activity where you feel closest to God. Dedicate time regularly to be in this space, fostering a deeper connection and listening to God's voice (Psalm 91:1-2).

4. **Declutter Your Mind:** Our minds can be noisy places. Learn to declutter your thoughts, write down your worries, and consciously hand them over to God. This act of surrender can bring profound peace (Philippians 4:6-7).

5. **Clean Your Spiritual Environment:** Surround yourself with positive influences and stay away from toxicity. Your spiritual journey is personal, so don't be swayed by others' choices or expectations (Proverbs 13:20).

AFFIRMATIONS:

1. My mind is open to receiving instructions from God.
2. I move and work with God's timing.
3. I run with purpose in every step and my best days are still out in front of me!

Chapter 3

Being Still

Being still isn't synonymous with inaction or passivity. Rather, it's a profound state of calm and trust, particularly in the face of adversity. Imagine standing in the heart of a storm, wind howling around you, rain beating down, and yet in your heart, there's an unshakeable calm. That, to me, is the essence of being still. The scripture calls us to stillness. Psalm 46:10 declares, 'Be still, and know that I am God; I will be exalted among the nations, I will be exalted in the earth!'

Trust is the anchor of stillness. In the biblical narrative,

Abraham provides a beautiful illustration of this. When God told him to leave everything familiar behind, he didn't resist, negotiate, or ask for a detailed roadmap. He trusted. His journey wasn't without its challenges, doubts, and moments of impatience. Yet, even when the promises made to him seemed physically impossible, Abraham's trust in God remained, enabling him to be still amidst life's uncertainties.

Consider the waves of the sea. On the surface, they might be wild, but dig a little deeper, and there's a remarkable calm. Our lives mirror this duality. On the surface, we face the chaos of our daily routines, challenges, and unexpected setbacks. But beneath that, in the depths of our souls, we have the capacity for an incredible stillness, a trust that no matter how fierce the storm, there's a force greater than any challenge we might face.

'The Lord will fight for you, and you shall hold your peace' (Exodus 14:14). This verse directly links to the concept of surrendering control, as it encourages trust in God's intervention and protection. It reassures that in moments of stillness and peace, God is actively working on behalf of His people, affirming that they need not fight their battles alone. This aligns with the idea of finding freedom in surrendering to a divine plan that surpasses our understanding.

When the winds of life threaten to toss you around, remember Abraham. Remember that deep beneath the waves, there's calm. Choose trust over doubt, faith over fear, and in the midst of the storm, be still.

Hearing God in a Noisy World

Today, with so many things buzzing around us, how do we hear God's quiet voice? It's not easy to pick out God's words when life is loud. Yet, it's so important.

First, we need to make a good space for the Holy Spirit to talk with us. Our minds are like a battlefield, with thoughts coming and going all the time. The devil often tries to talk to us, and sometimes even through us. So, there's a lot of noise in our heads. That's why I said we need to set aside time for God.

Three years ago, I decided to spend one hour each day just with God. Between three and four in the afternoon, I'd sit in my room, away from the world. I wasn't asking God for things. I just wanted to listen. We all have things we want, but sometimes, it's good to ask God what He wants from us.

Often, we only talk to God. We don't give Him a chance to answer back. We need to make time to hear Him. Today, with phones and tablets everywhere, it's hard. We wake up and look at our phones. We might spend hours on them. But finding even a short time for God can be tough.

To really hear God, we need to be calm. We need to clear our minds. The devil's voice can be loud. He talks a lot. But God? He's often quiet. He doesn't shout. So, if our minds are full of other things, we might miss what He's saying. 'Rest in the Lord, and wait patiently for Him; Do not fret because of him who prospers in his way, Because of the man who brings wicked schemes to pass' (Psalm 37:7).

This verse aligns well with the idea of finding quiet moments to hear and know God. It speaks to the act of resting in the Lord, finding tranquillity and patience in His presence, which can often be best achieved in quietness and stillness. By choosing to step away from the noise and busyness of life and not being preoccupied with the apparent success of others, especially those with ill intentions, we open ourselves up to divine communication and a deeper understanding of God's character and will.

Cultivating Stillness

In today's bustling world, where our minds are constantly filled with chatter, how do we find a moment of stillness?

Nowadays, our lives revolve around screens. Be it phones,

tablets, or computers, they dominate our attention. Conversations have become digital, and face-to-face interactions are a rarity. Things weren't always this way. Yet now, it's challenging to find even a brief moment of stillness in our packed schedules.

However, I've learnt that if you truly want to hear God's voice, you have to make an effort. It's not about finding the time; it's about making the time. Creating a no-phone zone, even for just an hour, can work wonders. And as you get used to it, you might find yourself gradually increasing that quiet time.

What we need now more than ever is not just a fast from food, but a fast from our devices. A 'digital detox' of sorts. This is essential because we need to give God room to speak. If our minds are always occupied, how can we discern His voice?

Think about it: sometimes, God speaks to us in dreams. These dreams can be powerful messages—revelations even. But if we jump straight into our daily digital routines upon waking, we risk forgetting these insights.

I remember my time at a strict school, where our mornings began with a silent walk to the chapel. No greetings, no chatter, just a silent communion with God. It taught me the importance of prioritising God above all else, even before greeting the people around me. That discipline shaped me, reminding me that God always comes first.

Benefits of Stillness to Spiritual Growth

Being still is more than just an act; it's a testament to spiritual maturity. When you can remain calm amidst a storm, it's a clear sign you're advancing in your faith journey. Here's a personal reflection to put it in perspective.

I once battled with bitterness and an inability to handle situations properly. Though I had valid points to make, my approach often caused unnecessary disagreements, especially with my siblings. Even when I was trying to guide them rightly, my impatient manner meant no one would listen, regardless of the truth in my words. Each time such confrontations occurred, I'd feel immense anger and regret. 'Why wasn't I still?' I'd ask myself. This repetitive cycle of bitterness stunted my spiritual growth.

In essence, being still means processing things without immediate emotional reactions. Even if someone's words seem outrageous or hurtful, taking the time to listen and process is vital. Speaking out of anger often just escalates issues.

Years of struggling with anger taught me this hard truth. When I reacted impulsively, I'd utter words that later haunted me with guilt. Each time I lost my cool, I felt like I was going in circles, not progressing spiritually. Bitterness is a heavy burden, replaying past events over and over, leading to an inability to forgive and move forward.

Then she said, 'Sit still, my daughter, until you know how the matter will turn out; for the man will not rest until he has concluded the matter this day' (Ruth 3:18). In the context of the story of Ruth, this verse demonstrates how stillness can indeed be beneficial. Naomi advises Ruth to wait, to be still, and after Ruth has followed Naomi's instructions in approaching Boaz for protection and to fulfil the role of the kinsman-redeemer. Ruth's stillness is a form of trust and patience, showing her faith in Naomi's wisdom and in Boaz's sense of duty and honour.

By embracing stillness, Ruth shows a controlled, patient attitude, which is crucial in her situation. Instead of being impulsive or trying to take control of the situation, she waits to see how events will unfold. This choice to be still ultimately leads to a positive outcome, as Boaz acts honourably and swiftly to redeem Ruth, which not only secures her future but also leads to her becoming part of the lineage of David and, ultimately, the genealogy of Jesus Christ.

In spiritual terms, Ruth's stillness before action is illustrative of a broader principle. By being still, we acknowledge that we do not have ultimate control, and we open ourselves to the workings of a higher plan. This act of stillness before God can lead to spiritual growth as we learn to trust in a power greater than ourselves and develop patience and understanding in our relationships and circumstances.

How Stillness Helps in Overcoming Life's Challenges

'And the Lord will take possession of Judah as His inheritance in the Holy Land, and will again choose Jerusalem. Be silent, all flesh, before the Lord, for He is aroused from His holy habitation!' (Zechariah 2:12-13). These verses culminate in a call for silence before the Lord, a silence that reflects reverence and awe as God moves to act on behalf of His people. The stillness here is not merely about being quiet; it implies an active cessation of human activity and anxiety, a pause in our own endeavours to acknowledge and make room for the workings of the divine.

In the context of overcoming challenges, this kind of stillness can be incredibly powerful. It allows for a space in which we can set aside our own efforts and struggles, look inward, and renew our connection with the Lord. By being still, we acknowledge that the ultimate resolution to our challenges comes not from our own actions, but from the power and presence of God. It's in this stillness that we can find the strength and wisdom to navigate the difficulties we face.

The power of stillness is found in Zechariah. It shows that by embracing stillness and introspection, we become more attuned to God's guidance and presence, which equips us to handle life's challenges with a clearer mind and a steadier heart.

Some years ago, I had a vivid dream. In it, a fierce wind transported me to my father's house, where I saw him lifeless. Amidst the mourning, someone mentioned that someone was responsible. But I, guided by an inexplicable force, lay on my father, breathed into him, and brought him back to life. It felt miraculous. When I woke from the dream, I spent time in prayer, seeking guidance from God, instead of immediately rushing to the distractions of my phone or day-to-day concerns. I needed that stillness.

Soon after, my mother called with distressing news that mirrored my dream. My father was gravely ill. Rather than panic, I felt an inner calm. I remembered the dream and the actions I took. I told her, 'Send him to me.'

When my father arrived, before seeking medical intervention, I took a spiritual route. I breathed into him, just as I did in my dream, believing in the healing power of faith. Only then did we proceed to a nearby Catholic hospital. Some might have opted for more renowned medical facilities, but I felt at peace with our choice. After all, I believed the most significant battle, the spiritual one, had already been won.

Remarkably, my father's health improved drastically. In a heartwarming turn of events, he asked me to make him new clothes, echoing the very words he had said in my dream. The spiritual significance wasn't lost on me. I had him clothed anew, symbolic of his renewed life.

Today, about a decade later, he's not just alive but thriving. This experience taught me the power of stillness. Had I not been still that morning after the dream, had I immediately lost myself in the digital world or daily chores, perhaps I wouldn't have recalled the dream when my mother's call came. But because I paused, reflected, and prayed, I had the clarity to act when the real-life challenge mirrored my dream. Try it; it will work for you.

AFFIRMATIONS:

1. I'm still because I know that He is God, and I am transformed by my encounter with Him.
2. I'm a child of the most high God. I hear from Him. I carry His DNA.
3. I'm established as a person by God, holy to Himself, for I keep the commandments of the Lord my God, and I walk in His ways.

Chapter 4

The Consequences of Disobedience

The ripples of disobedience, like stones cast into a still pond, echo through time, shaping the course of history and the souls of men. It's a theme that is both ancient and deeply personal, interwoven through every chapter of humanity. As I contemplate the biblical chronicles of those who defied God, I find myself reflecting on my own choices, the times I've resisted His will, and the inevitable repercussions that followed.

The story begins in the beautiful landscapes of Eden. The paradise God designed, where Adam and Eve, the very first humans, dwelt. Their intimacy with God was unparalleled, and yet, one act of defiance changed the course of mankind forever. They tasted the forbidden fruit, a choice that bore consequences not just for them but for all of humanity. In Genesis 3:6, addressing Eve, God declared, 'I will greatly multiply your sorrow and conception. In sorrow you shall bring forth children; your desire shall be for your husband, and he shall rule over you.' This decree, a result of their rebellion, reverberates through time, touching lives even today.

To Adam, God proclaimed in Genesis 3:17, 'Because you have heeded the voice of your wife, and have eaten from the tree of which I commanded you, saying, "You shall not eat of it": Cursed is the ground for your sake; In toil you shall eat of it all the days of your life.' Herein lies the birth of struggle, of man's arduous relationship with the land. The sweat of the brow, the labour of hands—these are the daily reminders of that one act of disobedience in Eden.

But they were not alone in their defiance. King Nebuchadnezzar's pride led him astray. God, in His divine justice, humbled the mighty king, causing him to roam the forests, eating grass like a beast. This humbling account, vividly depicted in the book of Daniel, chapter 4, verses 25 to 37, serves as a stark reminder of the perils of arrogance and the consequences of straying from God's path.

And then there was Cain, whose jealousy ignited a rage so profound that it led him to commit the first murder. By slaying his brother Abel, Cain ushered in a new kind of darkness into the world. His punishment? A life of wandering, marked by the weight of his guilt.

But not all acts of disobedience were as overt. Lot's wife, in a fleeting moment of curiosity, looked back against God's command and was turned into a pillar of salt. A simple act, yet it bore significant consequences, as recounted in Genesis chapter 19, verse 26.

And as Galatians 6:7 so aptly reminds us, 'Do not be deceived, God is not mocked; for whatever a man sows, that he will also reap.' Disobedience, in any form, has its repercussions. Just as a farmer reaps the harvest of the seeds he plants, so, too, do we reap the outcomes of our choices. When we sow disobedience, we harvest its consequences.

The Divine Nature of God's Guidance

Disobedience, in its essence, creates a chasm between us and God. When He nudges us towards a path or whispers guidance into our hearts, it's out of pure love and foresight. But God, in His boundless wisdom, allows us free will. He doesn't force us to tread His chosen path. Instead, He stands by, patiently watching as we make our choices.

A Life in Crisis

When we defy God's counsel, the effects are profound. Our lives become riddled with challenges, like a ship lost at sea without its compass. Things we pursue crumble, leaving us in a state of bewilderment. We grapple with doubt, even questioning God's very existence. It's a cascading effect: one wrong choice leads to another, each further distancing us from the divine. I've always believed, as I've shared previously, that life without Christ is riddled with crises. When we turn away from Him, we inadvertently invite chaos.

More recently, I had two dreams prior to leaving my brother's place for Brentwood and staying at another residence. These dreams again show the importance of obeying God.

The first dream involved my search for a house. In it, a woman led me to a residence that, to my dismay, was overrun with weeds and tall grasses. This dream seemed to symbolise a situation fraught with difficulties and discomfort. The second dream, occurring just a day before I departed from my brother's house, vividly depicted me returning to an old house where I lived about 20 years ago. This house represented pain and negativity, conjuring feelings of agony and distress.

These dreams transpired just as I had been praying for accommodation. When the offer came from the lady in Brentwood, it seemed opportune, prompting me to accept it hastily. The first dream, where the woman guided me to a house full of weeds, eerily mirrored my encounter with the lady from Brentwood, who appeared kind and offered me seemingly promising accommodation. This dream warned me of the deceptive nature of this offer, indicating that the place would not be conducive for me—spiritually, emotionally, or physically draining.

The second dream, depicting me moving back into an old, painful house, seemed to foretell my eventual return to my brother's house. It served as a metaphor for the cycle of leaving and returning to a place of discomfort.

Despite the significance of these dreams, I refrained from discussing them with my mentor, whom I usually consult about such profound dreams. My eagerness to leave my brother's house led me to ignore these prophetic warnings. In retrospect, the dreams were a clear indication of the challenges I would face and the eventual return to my brother's place, where I resided for a season.

A Personal Story of My Mother

To illustrate the profound consequences of ignoring God's directives, I recall an incident involving my dear mother. She was diagnosed with pancreatic cancer while here in the United Kingdom. Despite the best medical attention, her condition deteriorated with each passing day. In my heart, I felt an overwhelming urge to take her back to Nigeria to seek both traditional treatments and spiritual intervention. The feeling was so strong that I messaged my family, urging them to support this decision.

Yet, my pleas fell on deaf ears. They seemed convinced that the United Kingdom, with its advanced medical facilities, was our best hope.

Then, in what I believe was a divine intervention, I met a woman on a train journey from Bristol to London. This stranger, whom I'd later come to know as 'Mummy Blessing', was somehow intertwined with my mother's destiny. She was aware of my mother's condition and had even received messages nearly a year earlier urging that my mother be taken back to Nigeria. A covenant needed to be broken; spiritual healing was necessary.

However, my family remained steadfast in their decision. The days turned into months, and my mother's health further declined.

Despite Mummy Blessing's persistent prayers and her fervent pleas to me, the family's collective disobedience overshadowed any chance of divine intervention.

By the time my family heeded the call to return her to Nigeria, it was too late. My beloved mother passed away, leaving behind not just a void in our hearts, but also a painful lesson about the costs of disobedience.

Such experiences, as heart-wrenching as they are, serve as poignant reminders of the importance of heeding God's voice. It taught me that when God speaks, it's crucial to listen, even if it goes against the grain of popular opinion or logic.

My hope is that my family, and indeed all who read these pages, recognise the gravity of obedience to divine guidance. For in it lies not just our spiritual well-being, but also the very essence of our mortal lives.

The Chasm of Disobedience

Disobedience is not merely an act; it's the creation of a widening chasm. As one continues to defy the divine directives, an ever-expanding gap emerges between oneself and God. It's like quicksand—the more you resist, the deeper you sink. Soon, you find yourself lost, perched precariously on the fence of decision, with neither retreat nor advancement seeming feasible.

When God calls someone to a purpose, like ministry, and they flee from that calling, opting instead for the world's allure, like fashion or societal norms, they drift further from Him. This drifting isn't subtle; with each act of defiance, they're pulled deeper into the world's currents. And what starts as a gentle drift can quickly become a forceful pull, sweeping one into a life of confusion. For the chosen ones, comfort is elusive in such spaces. They feel perpetually out of place, for they are living against their divine purpose.

The Devil's Deception

The genesis of disobedience traces back to the serpent—the devil. When faced with a divine command, it's often the devil that sows seeds of doubt, offering tantalising alternatives. He promises clarity, but delivers confusion. He suggests that by defying God, one's eyes will be opened to new horizons, echoing his deceptive words to Eve. But in truth, he blinds you, making you see the world through his lens.

The devil doesn't just stop at the first act of disobedience. He guides you further down that path, constantly whispering in your ear. His voice, persistent and loud, often drowns out the gentle nudges from God. And while God occasionally sends reminders of the right path, the devil's noise can be overwhelmingly distracting. Remember, when you're on this path of defiance, it's not God's time you're wasting—it's your own.

Sadly, some traverse this path for years, even decades, never realising the gravity of their choices until it's too late. Some carry their unfulfilled destinies to their graves, having never accomplished their divine assignments. The world is littered with tales of such individuals. One such story that comes to mind is of a lady I once knew. Initially a gospel artist, she was drawn away by the world's allure, and the transformation was heart-wrenching. Her case serves as a poignant reminder of how the devil targets those with divine gifts, much like how he once was with his heavenly singing.

Inhibition of Spiritual Growth

The most profound impact of disobedience is the stunting of one's spiritual growth. Over time, one becomes unrecognisable, not just to others but to oneself. The identity gets clouded, and there's a profound sense of not belonging anywhere. This limbo is where many find themselves trapped by their own choices and the devil's deceit.

Disobedience of Destiny

Disobedience to God can significantly alter or delay the realisation of our destined paths. While God's vision for us is clear and unchanging, our detours driven by disobedience can lead to unforeseen delays. God, as the master of time, patiently waits for us to align with His plan. However, when we divert, the repercussions are not limited to us alone. Some individuals' destinies are intrinsically linked to ours. When we falter, their paths, too, can be affected, leading to a chain reaction of delays and misdirections.

This diversion from God's plan is often a result of the devil's trickery. He constantly seeks ways to divert us from our divine path, presenting distractions and temptations. When we yield to these distractions, we not only delay our own destiny, but also hinder others whose fate is tied to ours. This disobedience can lead to spiritual confusion, making us vulnerable to further distractions and deviations. The devil capitalises on this weakened state, further wounding our spirit and those connected to us. It's essential to recognise these detours and realign with God's plan, not just for our sake, but for those whose destinies are interwoven with ours.

Disobedience doesn't only affect purpose, but it can affect the lives of others. There's a man I have known for many years, as we're from the same state. During the pandemic, he proposed to me while he was in the United Kingdom and I was in Nigeria. Given our long-standing familiarity, I accepted his proposal. We began making plans for our future together. However, due to the sudden lockdown, he couldn't fly to Nigeria as planned. The distance began to strain our relationship, and over time, I realised he wasn't supportive of my aspirations and dreams. Recognising these differences, I decided to end our relationship but wished to remain friends.

A couple of months later, he informed me he'd found someone else. I wished him well and hoped for his happiness. However, about a month after this, I had a distressing dream. In it, I saw him in a mansion he was building in his village, which I had previously visited to help with furnishing. He was seated on a balcony in a wheelchair, appearing frail and skeletal. This image was in stark contrast to his robust physique. The dream evoked painful memories of my mother's final days. In the dream, he was saying, 'Chidimma, why did you allow me to come here?' He was in tears. I was filled with regret, questioning why he had returned to the village.

When I woke up, I made the mistake of not sharing my dream

with him. Given his spiritual inclination, he would have taken it seriously. Two weeks later, I received a heart-breaking call: he had passed away. He had travelled to Nigeria to pay a dowry for his new bride and had conducted a housewarming ceremony for his new mansion. Shortly after returning to the United Kingdom, he collapsed at work and tragically passed away.

His death weighed heavily on me. This felt like an unconscious form of disobedience. I felt an overwhelming sense of guilt for not sharing my dream with him, thinking it might have changed the course of events. A spiritual mentor of mine warned me never to keep such dreams to myself in the future. The look in his eyes in the dream seemed to ask, 'Why did you allow me to come here?' and it haunts me. Even today, the pain and guilt remain fresh in my heart, and I deeply mourn his loss.

Reversing the Consequences of Disobedience

Disobedience's consequences, while severe, can undoubtedly be reversed. God's grace, patience, and boundless love ensure that those who genuinely seek redemption find it. It's written, 'If my people, who are called by my name, will humble themselves and pray . . . I will heal their land.' This healing isn't just physical but spiritual, mending the damage done to our hearts, lifestyles, and souls.

The Consequences of Disobedience

Consider a recent personal experience. A disagreement with an older brother over his well-being led to harsh words exchanged. In the aftermath of that argument, it became evident that perhaps the approach was wrong. While the intention was rooted in concern, the delivery was perceived as overbearing. A moment meant to be an act of love was transformed into a rift. Yet, by taking time to reflect and accepting responsibility, an apology was extended. It's a small instance, but it mirrors our relationship with God. We may have good intentions, yet our actions might deviate from God's plan for us.

The reversal requires an honest introspection. We must acknowledge our missteps and disobedience, accepting responsibility rather than casting blame. It's easy to question God's fairness when faced with the outcomes of our actions, but it's crucial to remember that during our moments of indulgence, God was still there, offering guidance and waiting for us to listen.

An essential step towards mitigation is repentance. By approaching God with a genuine, contrite heart, we find not just forgiveness but restoration. God's mercy is infinite, and no matter how long we've strayed, His arms remain open, ready to welcome us back. By acknowledging our wrongs, seeking forgiveness, and committing to a renewed path, we not only repair our relationship with God, but also rekindle our divine purpose. In this renewed state, our true assignment, our true destiny, can truly commence.

Lessons from Moments of Disobedience

1. **Value of Experience:** Every act of disobedience, no matter how regretful, can offer a profound lesson. The failed marriage serves as a testament. Disobedience may lead to pain, but it can also guide us towards self-awareness and personal growth.

2. **Acknowledgement Is Crucial:** Recognising our mistakes is the first step towards redemption. Instead of casting blame elsewhere, we must accept our responsibility. It's not about faulting God; it's about accepting our own missteps.

3. **The Power of Repentance:** Once we acknowledge our sins, true repentance follows. This paves the way for genuine communication with God. By asking, 'What next, Lord?', we demonstrate our readiness to realign with His path.

4. **Trust in Divine Timing:** Life's adversities teach us patience and faith. God controls time and season, so even when His plans seem challenging, they are always for our best. It's a lesson in unconditional trust.

5. **Embrace Godly 'Foolishness':** Being 'foolish' for Christ means prioritising His ways over worldly views. It's about valuing eternal truths over temporary pleasures.
6. **God's Ever-Present Nature:** Even in our lowest moments, God is beside us. His love is unwavering, and He is always ready to guide us back. He's not distant, but deeply involved in every chapter of our lives.
7. **Unbreakable Bond of Love:** Our connection to God is fortified by love. Despite our disobedience, this bond remains unshaken. Like a parent waiting for a wayward child, God's arms remain open, offering forgiveness and renewal.

The journey from disobedience to redemption is filled with invaluable lessons. Each step, whether it's the pain of realisation or the joy of reconnection, shapes our spiritual path. By embracing these lessons, we not only find our way back to God, but also discover a deeper, more meaningful relationship with Him.

AFFIRMATIONS:

1. I'm chosen by God, holy, dearly loved, and called by God.
2. I'm the branch of the true vine, a channel of His life.
3. I'm chosen and appointed by Christ to bear His fruit.

Chapter 5

Desert Training

'*Light Through the Dark Desert*', the subtitle of this book, isn't just a poetic metaphor; it's a journey. A journey that each one of us embarks upon, knowingly or unknowingly. And it's impossible to embark on 'desert training' without first confronting the desert itself.

The desert, in a spiritual context, is more than just a barren wasteland. It symbolises a period of testing, refining, and growth. You cannot truly grow if you're always atop the mountaintop, basking in the sun. True growth, the kind that transforms and strengthens, occurs in the valleys, in the moments of sadness and discouragement. It is when we are most vulnerable, most raw, that we have the best opportunity to evolve and mature.

God uses our emotional lows, our desert experiences, as materials for our spiritual development. It's during these moments when Christians often feel abandoned, left to wander the vast expanse of their doubts and fears. Darkness prevails, and it's easy to question God's intentions or even His very existence. But remember, every desert has its dawn.

The desert is a place of isolation, testing, and, yes, sometimes chastisement. But it's also a space for profound cleansing and deep introspection. Think of the children of Israel wandering through the wilderness on their way to the Promised Land. They faced hunger, fatigue, and doubt. Yet, even in their darkest hours, God provided manna, sustaining them and proving His unwavering love and commitment.

The desert, vast and unyielding, beckons with its deafening silence, a place where the soul is laid bare, devoid of all pretence. In its vast expanse, it becomes a training ground, a crucible for refining the spirit. There, stripped of pride and comfort, I found myself grappling with the core of my very existence.

Loneliness is the desert's anthem, a song sung by the winds

that sweep its dunes. There, you find yourself abandoned, cast adrift by the world. In the midst of this desolation, be assured that His *'Light Through the Dark Desert'* will shine—the unwavering presence of God. This is the desert's paradox, a place of profound solitude where you are never truly alone.

In the desert, patience is your tutor. God's instructions, often cryptic and confounding, require one to wait, to listen, to trust. There's a lesson in the stillness, a reminder that true obedience demands patience. The desert doesn't yield its secrets easily. Here, faith is both the challenge and the reward.

Facing abandonment in the desert, one realises that momentary rejection is sometimes divinely ordained. When the world turns its back, it's often God's way of drawing you closer, teaching you to depend solely on Him. It's a painful lesson, but one that carves a deeper reservoir of faith within.

In the desert's vast theatre, prayer becomes your lifeline, the tether that binds you to the Divine. It's here that praise takes on new meaning. It's easy to sing when life is replete with joys, but in the desert? Here, every note is an act of defiance, a testament to undying faith even in the face of adversity.

Ironically, it's in the desert's harsh embrace that you learn the power of gratitude, the art of praising God even when every fibre of your being rebels. Obedience, here, isn't just about following commands; it's about surrendering to a higher will, even when it seems counterintuitive. The desert teaches you that sometimes, you need to decrease so that God can increase, to diminish so that He can take centre stage.

The desert is no ordinary place. It's a spiritual forge, moulding and shaping, reducing one to their essence so that they might emerge stronger, purer, and closer to the Lord.

Light in the Opaque Night

The desert, with its endless horizons and suffocating silences, seems to stretch infinitely. But even in its vastness, there's always a flicker of light. I found mine on the darkest night of my life.

One evening, as the weight of my cancer diagnosis pressed down on me, my heart felt as if it was giving out. I had just received chemotherapy, and I was weak. The monitors beeped incessantly, my blood pressure plummeted to alarming lows, and my heart rate faltered. The world seemed to blur and fade, and I felt an overwhelming sense of isolation. Despite being surrounded by machines and the sterile smell of a hospital, I felt more alone than I ever had before. The world seemed indifferent to my pain and my struggles.

As the night deepened, a profound weakness overcame me. I attempted to rise from my bed, driven by a basic human need. But my body betrayed me, and I crumpled to the cold floor. It was there, lying on that unforgiving surface, that despair consumed me. I felt abandoned by everyone: family, friends, the world. In that moment of utter desolation, I cried out to God, pleading for release. 'Take me,' I whispered, tears streaming down my face. 'I'm tired.'

But in the echoing silence, a voice whispered back, gentle but insistent. 'Abandon yourself for me.'

In that bleakest of moments, inspiration struck. Weakly, I reached for a pen and began to write. Words flowed from my soul, etching my pain, hope, and surrender onto paper. The song 'Abandon' was born. It became a testament to my journey, a beacon of light in the overwhelming darkness.

As the dawn's first rays pierced the horizon, I realised that God wasn't asking for a part of me; He wanted all of me. My struggles, my attempts to fit in, to follow the crowd—it had all been in vain. God wanted to be my guiding light, to shine through my darkest moments. And I had been pushing Him away, trying to do it all on my own.

The desert experience, though harrowing, was transformative.

No one can traverse its scorching sands and remain unchanged. It refines and renews, stripping away the superficial to reveal the essence beneath. And in that crucible, I was reborn. A fresh fire ignited within me, a renewed purpose. I had found my light in the desert.

In the heart of the desert's training, a song was born. Without the challenges of the desert training, this melody, echoing resilience and hope, might never have come to life.

Desert Training

Verse 1:

Oh Lord, the God of my salvation,
I have cried day and night before Thee.
Let my prayer come before thee, oh Lord,
Incline your ears unto my cry.
For my soul is thirsty for You, oh Jesus,
And my spirit longs for Your Word.
My heart yearns for You, Holy Ghost,
As I fall helplessly at Thy feet.
Then, do with me what thy will do,
Do with me what pleases You,
I abandon myself for You.

Chorus:

I abandon myself. I abandon myself.
I abandon myself for You.

Verse 2:

When the road looks so rough,
And the path so crooked,
When family and friends abandon me,
My strength fails me,
Answers to my questions seem far away,
Lost and lonely, I run to You.
Now do with me what Thy will do. Do with me what pleases You,
I abandon myself for You.

ABANDON by Chidimma D. Onuoha

Deserted in the Desert

During my desert journey, I experienced profound loneliness and challenges. After excitedly buying a car, I had to sell it just two months later upon being diagnosed with breast cancer. The subsequent chemotherapy drained me, and during this arduous period, the isolation from my loved ones was palpable. Despite gifting my father two cars and being hailed as his 'favourite daughter', he went silent when I needed him the most. Even in the UK, where three of my siblings reside, no one reached out. I vividly recall a desperate plea in our family chat room, expressing how I felt on the brink of death, but was met with silence.

It's in such moments of vulnerability that the devil seeks to strike, attempting to make one forsake all hope. Yet, this ordeal taught me resilience and the strength to confront adversity, including addressing cancer as the spiritual battle it truly is.

Losing Everything

I experienced a profound loss, the loss of all my belongings, all washed away by a devastating flood. I remember that fateful day vividly, as this was the time I was receiving cancer treatment. I had just stepped off the train, returning from the hospital, when my sister called me. She hesitated before breaking the news, as if struggling to find the right words.

'Something happened two days ago,' she began. 'I didn't know how to tell you.' I braced myself and urged her to continue. I had already endured my fair share of challenges.

'You know those things you stored at my house?' she asked. I nodded, my heart sinking with a sense of impending doom.

'Well,' she sighed, 'there was a massive flood in Lagos, Nigeria, two days ago. Everything got submerged. Your certificates, clothes, shoes, everything you had left at my place.'

I was speechless. My sister's words hung heavy in the air, and I fought back tears. But as I stood there, something unexpected happened. Instead of tears, a song of praise welled up inside me. It emerged from nowhere, and I couldn't comprehend how this melody took form.

This song, which encompassed three different languages—my native Ibo, Yoruba, and English—emerged spontaneously. I sang it out loud, heedless of the curious glances from passers-by. I sang with tears in my eyes, a peculiar blend of happiness, indescribable joy, and a profound sense of God's presence.

Here are the lyrics:

You Are Unkillable

Chorus

Okaka – The beginning and the end Kabiyosi ooo
– Royal Majesty Eledumare – God Almighty
Arugb Ojo – Ancient of days
Okaka – The beginning and the end Kabiyosi ooo –
Royal Majesty Eledumare – God almighty
Arugb Ojo – Ancient of days Chukwu oma – Beautiful God

Verse 1

There's an eruption of greatness
Glory like a cloud of fire
All over me Eledumare
The oil of gladness
For my mourning
Laughter for my pain Eledumare
Beauty for ashes
Double for my trouble
Garment of praise
For my sorrows
My joyful days are here
My joyful days are here Eledumare
Kabiyosi

In the face of loss, I learnt humility, and I found an unexpected gift, a song of praise that poured forth from my heart. I have recorded this song, a reminder of how, even in our darkest hours, there can be a glimmer of light.

God Calls Us to Be a Light

Amidst the storms and challenges you face, it's essential to remember that God has a unique purpose for you. Even in your darkest moments, He calls you to shine brightly for others, illuminating their paths and providing hope. While it may seem counterintuitive to be a light for others when you are engulfed in your own dark desert, it is in these trying times that your light can shine the brightest. I recall a particularly challenging day at the hospital during my own battle with breast cancer. On that day, amidst my own suffering and anguish, I encountered a woman who left an indelible mark on my heart.

As I waited for my own chemotherapy session, I noticed a frail woman accompanied by her son. She seemed worn out, defeated by her own battle with cancer. She was in conversation with a nurse, determinedly stating her wish to discontinue her chemotherapy.

She felt the treatment was worsening her condition, saying it sent her to the hospital after every session. She believed she was better off letting the cancer take its course than enduring the torture of the treatment.

Her son, visibly distressed by his mother's resignation to her fate, broke down. He looked at me, a stranger, asking why good people had to suffer. He could see his mother's spirit waning and felt helpless.

Moved by their pain, I approached the woman. I held her hand, looked into her eyes, and tried to instil hope, telling her that she could overcome her ailment. Initially resistant, she eventually relented, hugging me tightly, her tears mingling with mine.

Interestingly, when she learnt I was there for breast cancer treatment, she remarked I was 'lucky' since it was treatable. I realised then that her condition was likely more severe than mine. Before parting ways, I took her number, vowing to call her daily to offer encouragement. True to my word, I stayed in touch. Five months ago, she completed her chemotherapy. Today, she's doing considerably better, and thankful that God allowed me to be a light in the middle of someone's dark phase.

Light in the Operation Room

On the day of my mastectomy and breast surgery, as I regained consciousness in the recovery room, one of the nurses remarked with astonishment, 'I've never witnessed anything like this before. You were speaking in an entirely different language.' Another nurse chimed in, 'She was speaking in tongues until she fully awoke.' Remarkably, even in my unconscious state, I was praying in tongues. This experience brings to mind Romans 8:26, which states: 'Likewise the Spirit also helps in our weaknesses. For we do not know what we should pray for as we ought, but the Spirit Himself makes intercession for us with groanings which cannot be uttered.' In that moment, it felt as though a light had pierced through the dark ambiance of the operating theatre, guiding and protecting me.

In challenging times, God has consistently gifted me with songs to provide solace and strength. Following my mastectomy operation, I was once again blessed with a song titled 'Ayaya'. This instance was a testament to God's unwavering presence in my life.

You Are Unkillable

Verse 1

You raised me up
From grass to grace
Shut the grave for my sake
You became the fourth man in my fire
You moved me from lack to abundance
You gave me a voice, when I was so so so low
In the wilderness, you held my hand
And you walked me through it all Baba
That's why I say thank You, Chim imeela

Chorus:

Ayaya ime, imee – Thank You
Chim, ayaya, ime imee, iyoo – Thank You
my Lord Ayaya ime, imee
Ayaya ime, imee, iyoo (3x)

Verse 2

My heart is full of joy
For the king of kings has given me a new song
Now, I'm working on my high places
I'm equipped with all that I need
Now, out of my belly flows the rivers of living waters
I'm strong! I'm enlarged! I'm relevant!
His grace is speaking for me! I say ayayayayay
Ayaya ime, imee (God, thank You) Chim,
ayaya, ime imee, iyoo Ayaya ime, imee
Ayaya ime, imee, iyoo

AYAYA by Chidimma D. Onuoha

A Man Appears

While in the desert, Moses had a profound encounter with a burning bush, a beacon of light amidst the vast wilderness. This serves as a powerful reminder that even in our darkest moments, we should always seek the light. It affirms that hope and guidance can be found even in the most desolate situations.

I visited the A&E department two days post-surgery due to complications. Fluid had accumulated around the breast area, causing immense pain. Despite having two drains, one had ceased functioning, leading to the accumulation.

I arrived at the hospital at 8 a.m., and by 10 p.m., I was still waiting. The pain was unbearable, and I was quite vocal about it. It being a Sunday, there was no consultant or breast surgeon available. Feeling helpless, the staff wasn't sure how to assist. Around 9 or 10 p.m., a nurse approached, suggesting I go home and return the next day to see my breast surgeon. I protested, stating I'd already spent £40 on an Uber to get there and couldn't afford another trip home and then back the next day. When she indifferently suggested I take a train, I was flabbergasted. How could I, with two drains attached?

In utter frustration and pain, I created a scene, collapsing and rolling on the ground in agony. I cried out, lamenting the pain and the lack of understanding from the medical staff.

But before this scene unfolded, an unusual incident took place. A man I didn't recognise walked past my cubicle. He returned, stood in front of me, and began communicating using only hand gestures. He didn't utter a word but conveyed a message of reassurance, indicating that everything would be alright. Strangely, he gestured towards his left breast, the exact location of my mastectomy. For 15 minutes, he continued this silent communication. When he was done, he simply walked away. I had no idea who he was or where he came from. Who was this man? Was it an angel? He did bring light in my dark moment!

After my outburst, the hospital staff decided to move me to the oncology department for the night.

How God Sent a Mentor Into My Life

In life's darkest hours, it's not uncommon for one to feel isolated and alone. However, the Bible provides numerous examples of God's providence, illustrating that He often sends individuals into our lives to provide comfort, guidance, and support during trying times. One such poignant example is the story of Ruth and Naomi.

Naomi, originally from Bethlehem, found herself in the land

of Moab due to a severe famine. Over time, she faced the devastating losses of her husband and two sons. In the midst of this profound grief, Naomi decided to return to her homeland. She urged her two daughters-in-law, Orpah and Ruth, to remain in Moab and rebuild their lives. While Orpah heeded this advice, Ruth chose a different path. In an expression of profound loyalty and love, Ruth told Naomi, 'But Ruth said: "Entreat me not to leave you, Or to turn back from following after you; For wherever you go, I will go; And wherever you lodge, I will lodge; Your people shall be my people, And your God, my God"' (Ruth 1:16).

My path first crossed with Pastor Gideon's when I worked at Chevron. He was a supervisor for a different department. Our interactions then were limited mainly to the interdenominational fellowship services we had on Wednesdays, Fridays, and Sundays. He would occasionally preach, but we shared no personal rapport.

Years went by, and Pastor Gideon retired from Chevron. Our lives moved in different directions, and our paths seemed unlikely to cross again. However, fate had other plans. One day, I received a friend request from him on Facebook. I recognised him instantly and accepted. Our exchanges were brief, cordial, and sporadic, often limited to comments or likes on my posts.

Then came a period of intense personal struggle. I was about to undergo surgery, and the uncertainty of the outcome weighed heavily on me. Pastor Gideon reached out just days before my surgery, offering prayers and words of comfort. After the surgery, complications arose, and I was incapacitated for about a month. When I finally reconnected, Pastor Gideon was there, praying with me and offering solace.

Our conversations deepened when I was diagnosed with breast cancer. I was at a vulnerable juncture, and his unwavering support became my pillar of strength. Pastor Gideon transitioned from being a distant acquaintance to a mentor. The guidance he offered wasn't just about my physical health; he went deep, addressing the weight of bitterness and unforgiveness that had burdened my spirit.

What was most remarkable about our interactions was his intuitive understanding of my struggles. Often, during our long conversations, he would say something that directly addressed my current worries or challenges. His words always seemed to come at the right time, providing clarity and peace.

To say Pastor Gideon was God-sent would not be an exaggeration. At a time when I felt most broken, he became a beacon of hope and faith. Our relationship as mentor and mentee serves as evidence that sometimes, the most profound connections form when we least expect them. Light comes through at dark times if you trust God and the people He sends into your life.

Speaking from a Higher Realm

Romans 4:17 tells us about speaking things into existence and calling 'those things which be not as though they were.' This is from a higher realm and higher power. This principle became vividly clear during my journey in the desert.

In the midst of desolation, it's crucial not to articulate our feelings from the depths of despair, but to speak from a higher realm. During my ordeal, I felt the sting of abandonment, but it was in this very loneliness that I learnt to lean on God, the only true companion in the wilderness. One evening, as I lamented the absence of loved ones, I felt the whisper of despair suggesting that even God had forsaken me. Yet, a deeper voice urged, 'If the world has abandoned you, abandon yourself for me.'

True, the desert can be an agonising place of solitude, but it's also where profound communion with God occurs. It's the training ground for life's greater assignments, a season with a defined purpose and appointed time.

The voice of the adversary will try to drown out hope. I've been warned by many about the perils of chemotherapy, recounting stories of those who, despite initial victories, later succumbed to the disease. Yet, in the face of these daunting narratives, I've learnt to declare from a higher perspective. When doubt echoes that cancer will be my end, I counter with conviction, 'That is not my story.' I choose to speak life, to amplify hope, ensuring that my voice always rises above the whispers of defeat.

As a tradition on my chemotherapy days, I always kneel down to take communion, praying, 'Lord, as I come to receive my treatment, let whatever they inject into my body be transformed into Your precious blood.' I declare this from a higher realm. This ritual has become so well-known that even doctors and nurses are aware of it. After my final chemotherapy session at the hospital, I was inspired to write 'Yaweh'—a song from another realm.

Desert Training

Oyoyoyo oyooo
All glory to my Yaweh Oyoyoyo oyooo
All glory to my Yaweh

Jehova Jireh, my provider Jehova Rophe, my Healer
Jehova Nissi, my Banner Jehova Makadesh, my Sanctifier
Jehova Tsidkenu, my righteousness Jehova Shalom, my Peace
Jehova Rohi, my Shepherd
Jehova Shamma, my abiding presence

Yaweh, my Yaweh Yaweh, my Yaweh Yaweh, my Yaweh
You are my Yaweh, I give You praise

Emperor of the universe
The game changer, my soul provider
The Changer of all times and seasons
He that dwells in an unapproachable Light
The glory of Israel
My beautifier, my rising Light
From the blast of your nostrils, the Red Sea parted ways
When you smile, there's an earthquake in the world.
Conqueror! Conqueror!
Conqueror in everything, Conqueror in everything

YAWEH by Chidimma D. Onuoha

The Night of the Three Unusual Visitors

When you are in a desert place, there are things that will happen to you to train you and to see your reaction when they occur. In the year 2013, a remarkable and somewhat strange event unfolded in my life. It wasn't a dream; it was a very real and surreal encounter with three giant rats. This story is as true as it gets, and it all started during a period when I was seeking a deeper connection with God.

At the time, I often embarked on journeys to attend church programs or simply have quiet moments with the divine. On this particular occasion, I had just returned from my offshore job on a Monday. Without much delay, on Tuesday, I found myself heading towards Canaan Land, a massive church complex where I intended to spend some quality time with God. Canaan Land was a sprawling place, complete with hotels and accommodations for visitors like me.

The routine was simple, yet spiritually profound. My younger sister and I would check into one of the guesthouses within the church premises. We dedicated ourselves to a week of quiet contemplation and communion with the divine. This meant early mornings filled with prayer, fasting from 6 a.m. to 6 p.m., and hours spent reading the Bible and books written by various men of God. There was no room for talking, laughing, or any form of distraction; it was a time to focus solely on seeking God's presence.

For six consecutive days, every night at 2 a.m., we would wake up, take a walk around the church premises, and engage in fervent prayers, singing, and speaking in tongues. It was an intense spiritual experience that brought us closer to our faith.

After those six days of spiritual dedication, we returned to my home. However, what awaited us was something beyond ordinary comprehension. As I entered my house and switched on the lights, there they were, three big rats—not a dream, but a stark reality.

These weren't your typical house rats; they were unusually large, and they were clinging to the tiny cable of the air conditioner, almost as if they were holding hands. The sight was astonishing and surreal, given that I had never seen a single rat in my house before, and my home was quite spacious.

My younger brother, who was with me at the time, couldn't believe his eyes. He panicked and attempted to flee from the scene. However, I knew this was no ordinary occurrence. It was as if these rats were sent as agents of darkness to challenge my newfound spiritual strength.

I stood my ground and declared that we would not run from

this encounter. I saw them not as rats, but as demonic forces that needed to be vanquished. So, instead of fleeing, I took charge, and together with my brother, we confronted these strange invaders.

With determination, we managed to kill those three big rats that night. It was a battle, a spiritual warfare that played out in the physical realm. After that night, I never saw a rat in my house again, neither before nor after that peculiar encounter in 2013.

This extraordinary event served as proof that whenever you are called by God, there will be testing of your faith in the desert place. It was a reminder that sometimes, the challenges we face in life are more than they appear, and with the power of the Holy Spirit, we can conquer even the most unusual of adversaries.

In the Bible, Luke 10:19 tells us, 'Behold, I give you the authority to trample on serpents and scorpions, and over all the power of the enemy, and nothing shall by any means hurt you.' This truth was vividly demonstrated in the events that unfolded during this night.

The Transition of My Mother

The pain of losing a loved one is immeasurable, and the sorrow becomes profound when you witness their final moments. My mother's transition was perhaps the most heart-wrenching phase

Desert Training

of my life. She battled pancreatic cancer courageously, and for 15 months while she was here in the United Kingdom, the family became her pillar of strength. The weight of her journey bore heavily on my shoulders, and the culmination was the unforgettable moment when she breathed her last in my arms.

We took her back to Nigeria, and there, in my arms, she departed from this world. The image of her slipping away will forever remain etched in my memory.

Yet, in the face of such profound grief, my faith remained unshaken. The passing of my mother, while devastating, has not led me to question the divine. I firmly believe that her journey and mine are different narratives. Now, standing tall, I declare from a vantage point of unwavering faith that my story is yet to unfold in its entirety.

When the shadows of doubt creep in, suggesting that I, too, may meet a similar fate, I respond with resilience. I am more than my physical being. I am a woman with a purpose, on a divine assignment. My journey is far from over; the world awaits my voice. The trials I face, they target not my flesh but my voice. But this voice will not be silenced.

I confront my fears head-on, reminding myself and the adversities that they might have claimed a part of me, but they cannot possess what's truly valuable—my spirit, my voice, my purpose. I am more than the challenges I face. My body, the temple of the Holy Spirit, cannot be limited by mere ailments. I will rise, speak, and fulfil my destiny, always from a higher realm.

Warnings of My Mother's Spiritual Attack in Dream

In August 2017, prior to my mother's illness and subsequent passing, I experienced a profound dream. In this dream, I found myself at my father's house, where, for some reason, I felt a strong wind carry me into the compound.

Upon arrival, I noticed my mother's absence. I saw my father, a traditional ruler and a respected figure in our community, seated in his living room with two ladies. Intrigued and somewhat confused, I proceeded to my mother's room, only to find it empty. Her clothes and suitcases were neatly packed and set aside, an ominous sign that filled me with unease.

I called out to my mother repeatedly, but there was no response. Turning to my father for answers, I asked him about her whereabouts. His response was cryptic and unsettling. He looked at me with a peculiar expression, as if suggesting I was overstepping my boundaries, and then made a startling declaration that I would never marry. This was because of a vow or covenant he had made, which was a baffling and concerning revelation to me.

When I questioned the identity of the women with him, one of them claimed they were his wives. My father and the women then began laughing at me, a reaction that I found both disrespectful and hurtful. This was especially because we used to be very close, and so, even in the dream, I was startled by the hostility. In response, I started to pray in tongues, invoked the name of Jesus Christ, and called for a flood from all directions to engulf them. Miraculously, a flood swept into the room, carrying away my father, the women, and the furniture while I remained unscathed.

However, the dream ended without me finding my mother. Her room, with her belongings neatly arranged to one side, was a poignant reminder of her absence. As I continued to call out for her in the dream, I suddenly awoke.

Another Similar Dream

About four days later, shortly after my first dream, I experienced another vivid dream. This time, my father appeared, aggressively confronting me with a sense of foreboding. He reiterated his earlier declaration that I would never marry due to a vow he had made. His hostility was palpable as he chased me, vowing to harm me if I pursued marriage.

I pleaded with him, unable to comprehend his animosity. In the dream, my father had always been my best friend, so this sudden aggression was jarring and surreal. As the pursuit continued, I reached a point of exhaustion. No one came to my aid, despite my cries for help. It was then that I decided to confront him. As I continued running away, it was as though a voice spoke to me, telling me, 'You have what it takes to defend yourself'.

In a surprising turn of events, I found the strength to lift him up and throw him out of a window. This action revealed how light he actually was, contrary to the fear he had instilled in me. Following this, he fell and, in the dream, died. Still, in this dream, his death revealed the presence of his two sisters, my aunts, who came to the scene and accused me of killing their brother. They seemed indifferent to my plight, revealing that they had been in my mother's kitchen all the while. This detail was unsettling, especially considering the cultural significance of such a revelation in dreams from where I come from, often indicating impending death or serious illness. As they accused me, I also asked them why they had not come to my rescue when they saw their brother pursuing me. They were evasive and replied with, 'now you have killed him, hope you can now rest!' The entire situation was baffling to me, even in the dream, so I turned and asked them where they were coming from, as they were looking quite dressed. They said they were just coming from my mother's kitchen and were headed to see my maternal grandmother. In retrospect, this was interesting, as my grandmother had been dead for over 15 years at the time. Back in the dream, I rushed to my mother's kitchen, only to find it deserted, with her cooking utensils neatly packed away—a scene eerily reminiscent of her room in my previous dream. The aunts' indifference and their plan to visit my deceased grandmother only added to the dream's ominous overtones.

These dreams, filled with symbolic and distressing elements, seemed to foreshadow the challenging times that lay ahead, particularly concerning my mother's health. The vivid imagery and emotional intensity of these dreams left a profound impact on me, altering my perception and leaving me with a deep sense of unease and foreboding.

Travelling to See My Mother

Upon waking from these unsettling dreams, I was deeply troubled and immediately contacted one of my prayer leaders. I shared the details of the dreams: my father's declaration that I would never marry due to a covenant, the mysterious absence of my mother, and the foreboding statement from my aunt about visiting my deceased grandmother. These dreams were profoundly disturbing, prompting us to pray fervently.

Despite our prayers, I remained unsettled. By the 1st of September 2017, driven by concern, I decided to visit my parents, particularly to check on my mother. Before travelling, I called her and asked about her well-being. She mentioned her ulcer had returned, which alarmed me. I also inquired about my aunt, the one from my dream, but my mother seemed unaware of her current state.

When I suggested that something might be seriously wrong with my aunt, possibly even leading to her death, my mother dismissed my concerns, attributing them to my tendency to have prophetic dreams. I couldn't shake off the feeling that these dreams were significant.

Then, shockingly, the very next day, after sharing my dream with my mother, she called to inform me that my aunt had passed away. This news confirmed the ominous nature of my dream and intensified my need to understand the underlying meaning, especially the statements about marriage and the covenant mentioned by my father.

I booked the earliest flight home, and upon seeing my mother, I was startled by her appearance; she had lost weight and looked unwell. Although she attributed it to her ulcer, I suspected it was more serious. That night, I had a heart-to-heart conversation with my mother. I asked her about the circumstances surrounding my birth and any knowledge she had about covenants made by my father before our family embraced Christianity. My mother shared what she knew, but it was limited. The conversation was emotional, and at one point, my mother washed my face with water and blessed me as a gesture of protection and love. After a couple of days, I returned home, still processing the profound impact of these dreams and the recent events. The dreams had not only revealed hidden truths, but had also opened a path for deeper understanding and connection with my family's past and my own spiritual journey.

Forty-Thousand-Naira Dream

The dream that haunted me remained vivid and unsettling. On the 1st of September, I travelled back to my hometown, but the dream persisted, compelling me to return on the 15th of September. My aunt had passed away and was buried on a Friday, and though I couldn't attend the funeral, the dream about her continued to disturb me.

On the Saturday following her burial, a strange incident

occurred. I woke up early, at 5 a.m., with the intention of reading my Bible. It was a large print study Bible, which I had placed on my chest as I read. However, I must have dozed off into a state that was somewhere between sleep and a trance.

In this state, my aunt, who had just been buried, appeared to me. This experience was unnerving, and I often hesitate to share it due to its surreal nature. When she appeared, I greeted her as I used to when she was alive, calling her by the nickname we had for her. But her presence was so bewildering that I questioned it, reminding her she had passed away and been buried just the day before.

Despite this, she insisted on asking for 40,000 Naira, claiming she needed to tell me something important. When I asked why she needed the money and what she wanted to tell me, she revealed she had come to me specifically because I was the only one in the family capable of understanding and possibly helping. She then made a shocking revelation: she claimed that my father's house had been destroyed and there was blood everywhere. She urged me to look in a certain direction, and when I did, I saw a harrowing scene. My siblings and others appeared to be in chains, signifying turmoil and distress within my family.

Feeling alarmed and perplexed, I first attempted to contact my mother, but her phone was switched off. Consequently, I reached out to my spiritual director and prayer leader for guidance. They advised me to part with the 40,000 Naira, suggesting that God, who had revealed these events to me in the dream, would guide me on where to allocate the money. If no specific direction was received by the following day, I was instructed to offer it at the church altar.

Later that evening, as I was preparing to withdraw the money from an ATM, my mother called me. She had just returned from a church programme and shared an astonishing coincidence: at the programme, a man of God, unaware of my dream, had instructed her to sow a seed of 40,000 Naira. He specified that this was not for his church but should be given to women or a baby-related charity.

Stunned by this correlation, I immediately related my dream to my mother, emphasising the repeated mention of 40,000 Naira. I transferred the money to her account, instructing her to follow the man of God's direction and donate it as advised.

This peculiar sequence of events led to a significant development. Just two days later, my parents moved in with me for better medical care and check-ups. It was during this time that my mother was diagnosed with pancreatic cancer, and we later brought her to the UK for treatment.

The dream, with its vivid imagery of my family in chains and the destruction of my father's house, alongside the mysterious insistence on the 40,000 Naira, seemed to be a pivotal moment. It suggested a deeper connection between the spiritual and the physical realms in my family's life, highlighting the need for both prayerful and practical responses to our challenges.

In the dream, I witnessed a mysterious and intense scenario. I saw a woman who was not bound in chains but stood with a baby on her back. When I confronted her, she declared her intention to kill me. In the ensuing struggle, I first eliminated the child she carried and then her. Upon her demise, she transformed into a soft plantain tree, a species known for its softness in my culture.

Determined to uncover the truth, I insisted that something was hidden within the tree. I procured a cutlass and an axe, and upon slicing open the plantain tree, I discovered a coffin concealed within. To my horror, the coffin contained my younger sister, who had been experiencing mental health issues, leading me to suspect a spiritual rather than a physical cause for her condition.

In that moment of revelation, I realised the gravity of the situation. This wasn't a mere physical ailment; it was a spiritual attack on my sister's very essence. I swiftly took action, obtaining petrol and a lighter. Setting the coffin ablaze symbolised a fight against the spiritual forces at play.

As the flames consumed the coffin, a miraculous transformation occurred. My sister, whom we thought was lost, appeared at the gate of our house, alive and well. This was no coincidence; it was as if the burning of the coffin broke the spiritual chains that bound her.

The dream culminated in a powerful moment of liberation. As the coffin turned to ashes, I heard the sound of chains falling from my siblings' bodies, signifying their release from whatever spiritual bondage they were under. This was a moment of profound relief and joy for our family.

The mysterious woman's demise in the dream and the subsequent events were more than just figments of my imagination. They seemed to unravel deeper truths about the spiritual struggles my family was facing. This dream was a turning point, a revelation that led to a greater understanding and a path to healing. In this dream, the spiritual interpretation became clear: my mother had already been spiritually taken from us in 2017. The subsequent 15 months of her life were merely a prolonged struggle, devoid of hope for recovery. Despite her treatment in the UK as an international patient, which incurred substantial costs, it was all in vain.

Our family expended around 70,000 pounds on medical bills, a financial burden we willingly bore, unaware that her fate was already sealed.

This realisation struck me particularly hard on 17th September 2018, as her health continued to decline. I recall expressing to my siblings the futility of continuing her treatment in the UK. Based on the dream, I was convinced that her affliction was not just medical but spiritual in nature. I suggested taking her back home, as I believed she had been spiritually condemned already. This situation underscores the profound significance of obedience to divine revelations and visions, as they can offer insights beyond the scope of conventional understanding.

Obedience in the Desert Experience

The desert symbolises a spiritual wilderness, a place where faith is tested and where one's relationship with God is refined. During these trying times, obedience to God becomes paramount. As we recall the journey of the children of Israel, they often grumbled against the Lord, making their desert experience even more extended and challenging.

1 Samuel 15:22 is clear: 'To obey is better than sacrifice, and to heed is better than the fat of rams.' Obedience, while seemingly

straightforward, becomes strenuous during the desert experience. It's easy to complain, to question God's love, or to feel abandoned. However, genuine obedience accelerates our journey, making the wilderness experience more bearable and enlightening.

During the desert journey, distractions are abundant, and self-pity is a tempting escape. Yet, this is the exact time to dive deeper into the Word of God. Every challenge has its solution embedded in the scriptures. It's not a period for seeking pity or lamenting to others, but rather a time to commune personally with God, asking Him about the purpose of this journey.

God, in His infinite wisdom, speaks to those who listen. Obedience in the desert teaches patience. It's about remaining steadfast, even when the journey seems unending. Obedience not only shortens the journey, but makes it more fruitful.

Lastly, this training is aligned with God's love and purpose for us. Whom God loves, He chastens. He doesn't necessarily choose the qualified, but qualifies the chosen. If you've been chosen, expect refinement. But remember, this chastening is out of love, preparing us for a higher purpose, making us fit for the assignment He has in store for us.

The Power of Divine Guidance

I want to share another example that highlights the importance of obedience to God's guidance. When my mother fell ill, I accompanied her to the UK for her treatment. Although employed in Nigeria, I was fortunate that my boss supported my extended stay beyond the initial three weeks I had planned. He was American and reassured me that as long as I kept up with my work remotely, there was no issue.

I diligently worked from the hospital, ensuring my responsibilities were met. My boss praised my performance, encouraging me to stay in the UK as long as necessary. However, after entering the fourth month of my stay, human resources discovered I was working remotely, and I was abruptly dismissed.

But then, a divine intervention occurred. The night before my dismissal, I felt an overwhelming urge to transfer important emails, particularly those relating to my own health issues, to my personal account. This went against company policy, but I sensed it was crucial. I obeyed, and I thank God I did.

The next morning, I discovered I had been locked out of the company system and received an email informing me of my termination. In a state of shock, I consulted a friend who advised me to reach out to the general manager (GM). I was hesitant, as we weren't close, but I followed her advice. When I explained my situation to the GM, emphasising both my mother's illness and my own health concerns, he asked for proof. He then asked me if I had been communicating with the company's medical team. To this, I replied in the affirmative, as I had sent reports to the medical team, carrying them along on the journey. Chidimma Doris Onuoha.

This incident was one of the most amazing times when I enjoyed the power of His divine guidance because the previous night, I had worked till midnight. Just as I lay to sleep, at about 1 a.m., I was roused again to go and copy out this specific file on my correspondences with the medical team. It was indeed a strange prompting, as I did not know that I would be locked out of the company's accounts and system by morning. I obeyed the prompt regardless, and it was this obedience to His divine guidance that saved me on this occasion. If I had not obeyed, I would not have had any evidence to show the GM when I was asked.

The GM took up my cause upon presenting him with this evidence, advocating for my reinstatement. He highlighted my commitment and dedication to my work, and his efforts paid off. Not only was I reinstated, but I also received all the back pay owed to me. This experience underscored the profound impact of divine guidance and the importance of acting on it promptly, even when it seems to go against conventional norms.

Miracle of My Nephew's Birth

When my sister was expecting her second child, I was working offshore. A constant, nagging feeling consumed me, suggesting she wouldn't make it. Every instinct told me to rush to her side, but a sinister voice tried to dissuade me, hinting that I might see her for the last time. The thought of losing her was unbearable. When I finally met her, her pale appearance deepened my fears. She seemed unsure of herself, merely stating, 'I don't know,' when I inquired about her well-being.

That evening, I indulged in some red wine. It made me forget my primary mission: to pray for her. I woke up the next morning with a jolt, furious at myself for neglecting my duty. It felt like a spiritual battle was unfolding, and I was at its epicentre.

Determined, I asked my sister to join me in prayer. When she hinted she might be going into labour soon, I held her hands and declared, 'In Jesus's name, you will deliver safely, and both you and the baby will emerge healthy.' We prayed fervently from 9 p.m. until the early hours of the next morning. Afterwards, I went into the room to sleep, but as I lay down, a voice prompted me to get ready. Instead of sleeping, I dressed and sat down. Not long after, my sister's husband came in to let me know labour had started. We then took her to the hospital, her husband taking her to the hospital while I had her first child strapped to my back. At about 3 a.m., I felt the Lord instructing me to walk around the hospital seven times. I heeded this instruction, walking around the hospital, singing and praying in tongues. Shortly after, the doctor came and advised us to take her back home, as she was not fully dilated. However, we felt otherwise, and true to that feeling, not long afterwards, the doctor was called back, as she was fully dilated. I was invited into the labour room at my sister's request, and I continued to hold her up in prayers and the singing of praises.

The delivery was challenging, but my sister insisted I be present in the delivery room. As I sang and spoke in tongues, praying for her and the baby, the atmosphere was charged with faith and anticipation. She had informed the nurses beforehand that I should be the first to hold the baby and anoint him as soon as he was born. As the miracle baby arrived, I cradled him in my arms, continuing my prayers, grateful for the gift of life and the power of faith. This is the power of obedience to God— Chidimma Doris Onuoha.

Sustaining Faith Through Desert Times

Navigating through the desolate stretches of our spiritual journey, often termed 'the desert times', can be daunting. However, there are tools and practices to help us sustain our faith during these challenging periods:

1. **Speak from a Higher Realm:** Elevate your perspective. Address challenges not just as physical obstacles but as spiritual confrontations.

2. **Confront with Authority:** Don't remain silent when adversities or doubts assail you. Much like Jesus countered Satan's temptations with scripture, be equipped to rebuff the devil's accusations with spiritual truths.

3. **Feed Your Inner Man:** The desert period is a waiting time. While it's tempting to give in to desolation, it's crucial to nourish your spirit. Dive into scriptures, even when it feels challenging.

4. **Surround Yourself with the Right Company:** Engage with individuals who uplift and inspire you. Avoid those who drain your energy or foster negativity.

5. **Personal Experience with God:** Remember that the desert experience is deeply personal. It's a divine walk where

God prepares and moulds you. Keep distractions at bay and focus on this intimate communion.

6. **Stay Focused on the Promise:** Concentrate on the task and purpose God has set before you. Always keep an eye on the 'promised land', the spiritual destiny that awaits.
7. **Seek the Light Amidst Darkness:** In every desert journey, there is always a beacon of light. Search for it, cling to it, and let it guide you through the trying times.

By adhering to these practices, you can emerge stronger, more refined, and with a deeper connection to your faith from your desert experiences.

AFFIRMATIONS:

1. God has a purpose for my life.
2. I'm more than a conqueror through Christ.
3. I'm fearfully and wonderfully made.

Chapter 6

The Danger of Following the Crowd

A few months back, I wrote a song, and I forwarded it to my producer in Nigeria to craft the instrumentals. With the tune in hand, I headed to a nearby studio to lend my voice to the creation. As I reviewed the final piece, a nagging question repeatedly surfaced in my mind: could this song stand its ground against those of the renowned Nigerian gospel artists? Was my voice, my song, potent enough to compete with them?

As I grappled with these thoughts, trying to modify my voice, trying to emulate the sound of other popular singers, a profound revelation struck me. God's voice resonated, declaring, 'My daughter, I have not called you to entertain or perform. I have called you to minister.' The weight of this realisation was immense. Here I was, idolising other singers, aspiring to mirror their success, when in truth, God had a unique path charted for me.

This was my moment of clarity—I was veering off my spiritual path, trying to mould myself in someone else's image. I was following the crowd. But God's message was unmistakable: I am unique, designed for a distinct purpose. He urged me to remain unwavering, to tread the high road He had set for me.

What does it mean to follow the crowd? The Bible counsels, 'Do not be unequally yoked with unbelievers', indicating that aligning ourselves too closely with worldly ways can distance us from God.

Let's visit 2 Corinthians 6:14-18: 'Do not be unequally yoked together with unbelievers. For what fellowship has righteousness with lawlessness? And what communion has light with darkness? And what accord has Christ with Belial? Or what part has a believer with an unbeliever? And what agreement has the temple of God with idols? For you are the temple of the living God. As God has said: I will dwell in them And walk among them. I will be their God, And they shall be My people. Therefore, 'Come out from among them And be separate, says the Lord. Do not touch what is unclean, And I will receive you. I will be a Father to you, And you shall be My sons and daughters, Says the LORD Almighty.'

Societal norms and pressures can, indeed, distract us, leading us astray from our spiritual journey. Numerous voices compete for our attention, attempting to divert us from God's chosen path. It's crucial to remember that God has meticulously designed a unique journey for each of us long before our time on this Earth began. However, the allure of the crowd, the desire to fit into a mould that seems more 'successful' or 'accepted', can often blind us to our true calling.

In essence, while the path God has laid out for us may not always seem glamorous, it's essential to embrace our individuality and not lose ourselves in the discord of societal expectations.

The risk rooted in following the crowd is one of dependency. The moment you immerse yourself in the masses, you shift your reliance away from God, becoming increasingly influenced by the voices of many. This isn't just about spiritual allegiance; it's about intellectual autonomy. Your ability to think independently, to form your own viewpoints, becomes overshadowed by the prevailing consensus.

This herd mentality doesn't merely erode your spiritual

connection; it suppresses your unique voice. God, with his boundless wisdom, crafted each of us to be distinctive. Yet, in succumbing to the crowd, that divine individuality gets diminished. The outcome? An existence where you're continually trying to fit a mould, losing touch with your authentic self.

By aligning with the masses, you not only compromise your individual essence, but also delay your spiritual and life journey. Remember, you weren't created by God to merely blend in. You were designed to stand out, to lead others towards Him. But, by adhering to the crowd, you risk losing that unique voice—a voice intended to offer hope and be a beacon for others.

In essence, merging with the crowd doesn't just strip you of your identity; it deprives the world of the singular insights and gifts only you can provide. It's a dual loss—for you and for a world that misses out on your distinctiveness.

The Illusion of Temporary Satisfaction

I recall a chapter of my life where I became ensnared by the allure of worldly things, seeking temporary satisfaction by following the crowd. Take, for instance, my obsession with shoes. It may sound trivial, but it was a symbol of the larger issue. I owned more than a staggering 100 pairs, proof not of my love for fashion, but rather of my desperate need to fit in with the world's ever-changing trends. Every new release, every designer label, became a must-have. I thought these acquisitions would complete me, but the emptiness persisted.

In the professional realm, I was the epitome of success. I wore the title of a smart, young cost engineer with pride. Entrusted with millions of dollars for projects, I walked among the echelons of high society, my competence and confidence evident. Yet, beneath this facade lay a profound loneliness. At the end of the day, when the applause faded and I returned to the solitude of my home, the hollowness would engulf me. The glamorous life, the accolades, the shoes—none of it could fill the void.

This is not just a story; it's my reality. It's the narrative of how following the crowd only grants temporary contentment. In the company of the crowd, you might feel elated, but once you're alone, reality strikes hard. The emptiness resurfaces, reminding you of the hollow pursuit of mere worldly pleasures.

The scriptures echo this sentiment. Isaiah 8:11 speaks of the Lord's warning against walking in the ways of the masses. Furthermore, Exodus 23:2 cautions against following a multitude towards wrongdoing, emphasising the importance of remaining true to one's convictions rather than succumbing to the majority's influence. My story stands as a testimony to this timeless wisdom.

Thus, when you're ensnared in the trappings of following the crowd, an unsettling truth emerges: true satisfaction remains elusive. The only source of genuine contentment and fulfilment, especially for a Christian, is found in Christ alone. For those chosen by Him, life without Christ feels incomplete despite the fleeting pleasures the world may offer. So, while mingling with the crowd may provide a transient sense of gratification, it's just that—temporary. True, lasting satisfaction is found only in the embrace of Christ.

Do Not Fear Taking the Righteous Path

Embrace the journey that guides you to your divine purpose. For it is within this calling that you'll discover true fulfilment. Straying from this divinely appointed path may only plunge your life into turmoil. Such has been my experience. Romans 12:2 reminds us, 'Do not conform to the pattern of this world, but be transformed by the renewing of your mind. Then you will be able to test and approve what God's will is, His good, pleasing and perfect will.' There is a divine design for each of God's children. Recognise and understand this purpose early on. By adhering to God's plan and guidance, you find genuine peace. This is where authentic peace resides.

Delays from Following the Crowd

For a staggering 18 years, I fell into the trap of conformity, seduced by the allure of societal expectations. Let me take you back to my time at Chevron, where the siren call of materialism was impossible to ignore. The obsession was no longer about the work, but about superficial markers of success: designer labels, the latest trends, and the ceaseless competition of having the best of everything. Despite being on a contract, I was desperate to fit in, to measure up to the permanent staff.

Yet, in this race, I often wonder about the missed opportunities. How many souls could I have drawn closer to Christ? How much more of a difference could I have made in the house of God? The impact I could've had, the relevance I might've achieved in the eyes of the Almighty, all sacrificed at the altar of societal approval.

Every divine assignment has a time and place. When God has a purpose for you, He directs you towards it. Consider Abraham, whom God instructed to leave his homeland for a place of divine destiny. Our divine tasks are intrinsically linked to specific moments and locations. Yet, swayed by the crowd, we often lose sight of this. We get caught up in the transient, forsaking the eternal. I was no exception.

In my quest to blend in, I sacrificed my individuality. I silenced my unique voice, letting the deafening cacophony of the masses drown it out. The fear of the unknown, the dread of job insecurity in a challenging Nigerian job market, kept me chained. Even when God whispered promises of a brighter destiny, I hesitated. The divine path often seemed rugged and less appealing compared to the glittering highways of worldly success.

By chasing trends and trying to keep up, I lost a sense of who I truly was. I became a shadow, a reflection of others' expectations. This is the danger of following the crowd—it robs you of your essence, dims your light, and delays your destiny. The Bible warns us against being 'unequally yoked with unbelievers'. Yet, often, the crowd we find ourselves in doesn't share our beliefs. Seduced by the lure of temporary acceptance, we forsake our eternal mission.

Think about the countless souls yearning for guidance, those whose destinies intertwine with ours, waiting for our light to illuminate their path. Every time we succumb to societal pressures, we not only betray our true selves, but also those who depend on us. We're called to be lights, not mere reflections. Let's not lose ourselves in the crowd. Let's find our voice, our purpose, and embrace our unique journey with God.

The Story of Saul

In the First Book of Samuel, Chapter 15, we're presented with a powerful narrative that underscores the perils of following the crowd. Saul, the first king of Israel, was given a clear directive from God through the prophet Samuel. The command was straightforward: obliterate the Amalekites and spare nothing—man, woman, child, or beast.

Yet, when faced with the reality of the situation, Saul deviated from this directive. He spared King Agag of the Amalekites and chose to save the best of the livestock. These actions were in direct contravention of God's instructions. Why did Saul, with all his kingly authority and might, choose this path? The answer lies in his own admission: he feared the people and their opinions.

In 1 Samuel 15:24, Saul confesses, 'I have sinned. I have transgressed the commandment of the Lord and your words because I feared the people and obeyed their voice.' Here, Saul admits his fear of feeling left out, of not being part of the popular opinion, and the weight of societal expectations. He allowed the voices of the masses to drown out the voice of God.

This story is a poignant reminder for us. Saul's need for validation from his subjects and his desire to be accepted, celebrated, and revered led him to disobey a direct command from God. The cost was immense. Not only did it lead to Saul's eventual downfall, but it also severed his divine connection with God.

In our modern context, the pressures might look different, but the essence remains the same. The allure of following trends, seeking approval, or avoiding FOMO (fear of missing out) can sometimes sway our judgement. We may compromise our beliefs, values, and integrity for temporary satisfaction or acceptance. But as Saul's story warns us, the long-term consequences of such choices can be dire.

As we navigate the challenges of our times, let's remember the lessons from Saul. Following the crowd might offer temporary gratification, but it's our unwavering commitment to our principles, values, and, most importantly, to the divine directives that offer lasting fulfilment and peace.

Discernment Is Essential

To make the right choices in life, it's crucial to seek God's discernment about whom to follow and where to go. 1 John 4:1 declares: 'Beloved, do not believe every spirit, but test the spirits, whether they are of God; because many false prophets have gone out into the world.'

The Danger of Following the Crowd

I once mistakenly sought help from a dubious individual based on a friend's recommendation. This experience underscores the importance of seeking divine guidance and discernment, rather than merely following the crowd.

During a particularly challenging period in my life, I experienced a dream in which someone administered an injection to my head. Following that dream, I suffered from a relentless headache that lasted for three hard months. No day was free from the torment. In desperation, a neighbour directed me to a so-called 'spiritualist' or 'man of God'. Though she claimed he was powerful, upon my arrival, I quickly discerned he was far from divine. The setting was unsettling, not resembling a church, but rather a dim room adorned with peculiar images.

His appearance was disconcerting. He was a spiritualist. With a scant few teeth, each abnormally large and reminiscent of Dracula, I doubted if this was the person who could bring about my healing. Despite my reservations, he seemed to know about the injection from my dream, claiming it was an attempt on my life or sanity. Though I was reluctant, he convinced me to approach him, promising relief. He told me to remove my clothes, and I declined. To my surprise, he bit me on my head and removed a small stone, claiming to have removed the source of my pain. When he bit me a second time on my chest, claiming to remove another stone, I felt even more uncertain about his methods.

My condition deteriorated rapidly after that encounter. The already severe headache became excruciating. On a bus journey home, I lost consciousness. The next thing I remember was waking up in a church. The bus driver had contacted my childhood friend, whose number was the last I contacted—Amandi—who, in turn, took me to his church. To my surprise, the pastor's wife mentioned that the Holy Spirit had foretold my arrival. I spent three days at that church, surrounded by prayer and care, until I finally awoke, and God healed me. When you are in a dark place, it's dangerous to follow man—so follow God instead.

Resisting the Temptation to Follow the Crowd

In my journey, there have been innumerable moments of temptation, beckoning me to follow the crowd. Yet, I've found that true strength and clarity come from understanding oneself and prioritising spiritual well-being over societal pressures.

1. **Blocking Out Noise:** Over time, I realised the importance of distancing myself from distractions. I had to sever ties with certain friends, not out of animosity, but because our paths were diverging. It was imperative for me to surround

myself with individuals who supported my spiritual growth.

2. **Rediscovering Authenticity:** After the pandemic-induced lockdown, I had an epiphany. For the first time, I stepped into the office without the mask of makeup. To my surprise, I was showered with compliments. This experience reinforced my belief that authenticity and inner beauty are far more valuable than societal standards of beauty.

3. **Seeking Spiritual Growth:** There were times I succumbed to the allure of external validation. However, every misstep led me back to a conversation with God. I would pour out my regrets, asking for strength and guidance. This continuous dialogue deepened my connection with the divine.

4. **Understanding Purpose:** Our life journey isn't meant to be dictated by the crowd. It's essential to discern our individual paths and the unique assignments God has for us. By aligning with our spiritual purpose, we can find genuine satisfaction and purpose.

5. **Limiting External Influences:** The world is a cacophony of opinions and trends. However, it's vital to filter out the noise. For me, this meant exiting certain WhatsApp groups

and limiting my interactions with individuals who didn't contribute positively to my spiritual journey.

6. **Embracing Vulnerability with God:** I've learnt the importance of being open with God, discussing my fears, hopes, and even my mistakes. This openness has fostered a deeper bond and understanding of my spiritual journey.

7. **Recognising Individual Paths with God:** We must remember that our relationship with God is unique. While some might stray and face no immediate consequences, others, like me, feel the gentle chastisement of God when we deviate from our path. Recognising and respecting this individual relationship is paramount.

In conclusion, resisting the temptation to follow the crowd isn't about isolation but about prioritising spiritual well-being. It's about discerning which voices genuinely uplift us and which ones pull us away from our divine path. It's a journey of continuous reflection, learning, and growth.

AFFIRMATIONS

1. I am a member of a chosen race, a royal priesthood, a holy nation.
2. I am God's masterpiece.
3. I am complete in Christ.

Chapter 7

The Blossoming of Destiny in the Desert

On the 1st of December 2022, as the cruel clutches of chemotherapy worked on me, the world outside heard my song titled 'Chukwu' echo in celebration of God.

Here are the lyrics:

Ibo: Chukwu eee! Chukwu eee! Chukwu eeee!
English: God! God! My God!

Verse 1
Ibo: Chukwu, onye oma mkpuru obi m ooo
English: God, the love of my heart
Ibo: Chukwu moo, agu n'eligwe Chukwu
English: My God, the Lion of heaven and earth
Ibo: Mgbe ogbajuru doro, okwa gi ka m na-akpo
English: When I am overwhelmed with issues of life,
You are the one who I run to.
Chorus: Chukwu eee! Chukwu eee! Chukwu eeee!

Verse 2

Ibo: Udo asuru na mba, anu y ana mba ozo eee
English: One sound that shakes the whole earth
Ibo: Onye kwuru okwu na Jerusalem, omee na Capernaum
English: He who declared in Jerusalem and it manifested in Capernaum
Ibo: Uta gbawara ili eee, were turu ugo were lota
English: He who destroyed the power of death,
broke the chains of the grave and arose gloriously
Ibo: Ano m akpo gi Dike, agu na onwe ya Dike
English: I call You warrior, the Lion Himself! Warrior!

The Blossoming of Destiny in the Desert

Ibo: Asi na ibu ebube dike, msi na ikariri ebube dike

English: People call You warrior, but I say You are more than a warrior

Prior to this, I had heard the voice of God ask me to write Him a song about his healing power, but I hesitated. I asked back, 'But how can I write a song about your healing power in my current state?' It seemed to me like a huge paradox. The song I received was a song of praise and worship; it was meant to testify as a light of my faithfulness in the face of health challenges. As I debated this leading, my cousin, from the distant lands of Austria, rang me one day during my treatment. With a voice thick with emotion, she relayed a message: 'Auntie, Jesus says you should compose a song about His healing power.' At this point, I knew this was God speaking and so, in my moments of vulnerability, with feeble hands and a spirit unbroken, I penned down the lyrics. I looked nothing like the vibrant woman I once was, but the song was my testimony. It was my tune of hope. Even in this wilderness, amidst the desert of despair, I chose to praise. I chose to sing. Interestingly, when I went to the music studio to record, I had no lyrics written down. This was unconventional, as the ideal is to have the lyrics written down and then go to the music studio to perform from that. However, in my case, I recall just going into the booth and asking the Holy Spirit to take over me, and He did! It was afterwards that the lyrics were penned down. Here are the lyrics:

The Blossoming of Destiny in the Desert

Amen by Chidimma D. Onuoha

Verse 1

The power of the Holy Ghost is moving everywhere.

And the healing power of Jesus is present where you are.

He's moving everywhere, with healing in His wings.

I can see His creative miracles everywhere.

Now, He says right now, 'be ye made whole.

By my stripes, by my wounds, be ye made whole.

I am the Lord that heals thee, I'll make you whole.'

And you say, 'Amen, Amen, Amen!'

Amen! Amen! Amen! Amen! Amen! Amen! Amen! Amen!

Verse 2 (part of this verse is sung in my language – Ibo)

Ibo: Chukwu ahapughi nwa ya, na ala ndi nwuru anwu

English: God did not abandon His son in the land of the dead.

You Are Unkillable

Ibo: Chukwu ahapughi nwa ya n'ime ili

English: God did not abandon His son in the grave

Ibo: Ahu ya ereghi ure; oreghi ure

English: His son's body did not decay; He did not decay.

Ibo: Chukwu ahapughi nwa ya, n'ime ili

English: God did not abandon His son in the grave

So, He says, 'fear not,

I'll come through for you. I am the balm of Gilead,

The wounded Messiah.

I'll come through for you.

I open my wounds for you right now. Be ye made whole,'

And you say, 'Amen, Amen, Amen…'

Amen! Amen! Amen! Amen! Amen! Amen! Amen! Amen!

Ad libs

Now be ye made whole – Amen (John 5:9)

He says, be ye made whole – Amen

The blood makes you whole – Amen (Isaiah 53:5)

I will take sicknesses away from the midst of you – Amen

And the number of your days I will fulfil – Amen (Exodus 23:25)

I have redeemed you from every sickness and every plague

– Amen (Deut 28:61, Gal 3:13)

Amen by Chidimma D. Onuoha

The Blossoming of Destiny in the Desert

I will preserve you and I'll keep you alive – Amen (Ps 41:2)

You Are Unkillable (Light Through the Dark Desert)

I am the health of your countenance – Amen (Ps 43:5)
No more plague shall come near your dwelling – Amen (Ps 91:10)
I will satisfy you with long life – Amen (Ps 91:16)
I heal all your diseases – Amen (Ps 103:3)
I heal your broken heart and bind your wounds – Amen (Ps 147:3)
You shall not die, but live to declare the goodness of the Lord in the land of the living – Amen (Ps 118:17)
The eyes of the blind shall be opened – Amen (Isaiah 32:3)
The ears of the deaf are opened right now – Amen (Isaiah 32:3, 35:5)
The tongue of the dumb shall sing Amen (Isaiah 35:6, 32:4)
I will recover you and make you whole, say Amen (Isaiah 38:16) Be made whole!
Be healed of cancer!
Be healed of all infirmities! Be delivered!
Be liberated!

My destiny had more in store. The 7th of April, 2023, marked another milestone in my journey. Fresh from a 10-hour-long surgery on the 4th, where I underwent a mastectomy and reconstruction, battling with the threat of death, another song of mine found its way into the world. Titled 'Tetelestai,' which means 'It is finished,' the song was a declaration that my suffering was at its end.

Though I lay in a hospital bed, wracked with pain, my song echoed the sentiments of victory. 'It is finished.' The end of my suffering, the culmination of my pain, and the beginning of my renewed journey. Those who listened to its notes, felt its power, and joined in its chorus remained oblivious to my physical state. They did not know that as my song uplifted them, I was in the throes of a battle for my life. Here are the lyrics:

The Blossoming of Destiny in the Desert

Hey! I may not know what you're going through at the moment. I may not know what the situation looks like. I may not know the picture you see. I may not be able to feel your pulse.
But I know someone who felt your pulse even before you were conceived.
I know the Calvary man who redeemed us, even before we were born.

Oh Oh Oh, TETELESTAI Oh
Oh Oh, TETELESTAI Oh Oh Oh,
TETELESTAI Oh Oh Oh,
TETELESTAI

When the storm is raging, and you're standing on sinking sand -
Oh Oh Oh, TETELESTAI

Down in the valley of affliction and sorrow -
Oh Oh Oh, TETELESTAI

Remember that the sacrifice has been completed on the cross - Oh Oh Oh, TETELESTAI
And now we are free, truly free - Oh Oh Oh, TETELESTAI He says 'TETELESTAI'
He says 'TETELESTAI'
Jesus says 'TETELESTAI' Father says 'TETELESTAI'
IT IS FINISHED 'TETELESTAI'

TETELESTAI (It Is Finished) by Chidimma D. Onuoha

You Are Unkillable

All my problems 'TETELESTAI' Odogwu! Odogwu!

'TETELESTAI' TETELESTAI TETELESTAI

Jesus m eee! Jesus m eee! Jesus m eeeee!

He was bruised for our transgressions!

The chastisement of our sins was upon His shoulders!

And by His stripes, we are made whole! IT IS FINISHED! TETELESTAI!

You died on the cross to set me free.

You paid the price on the cross of Calvary. Jehovah m eeee, it's only you I know.

Onye nwùrù n'elu obe, wee gbagbùta m na njò - Oh Oh Oh, TETELESTAI

Your sacrifice has brought me victory: Oh Oh Oh, Tetelestai

You've lifted my feet, placed them on solid ground: Oh Oh Oh, TETELESTAI And now I can shout, 'TETELESTAI' Oh Oh Oh, TETELESTAI

To my fears - TETELESTAI To my worries - TETELESTAI Marital delay - TETELESTAI Barrenness - TETELESTAI Infirmity - TETELESTAI Poverty - TETELESTAI

Near success syndrome - TETELESTAI

Jesus says - TETELESTAI

Now forget the things of the past; remember them no more.

For He has done a new thing.

He has made a way in the wilderness and rivers in the desert. IT IS FINISHED! TETELESTAI!

Thank you for the freedom. Thank you for redemption.

Thank you for liberation.

Thank you for the cross.

I will praise you every moment of my life, Every second of the minute,

The Blossoming of Destiny in the Desert

Every minute of the hour, Every hour of the day, Every day of the month.

I will worship you - TETELESTAI

In the dark - TETELESTAI

In the wilderness - TETELESTAI Sickness - TETELESTAI

Nýanỳ a nìle - TETELESTAI Akòm ònù nìle - TETELESTAI Abùm ònù nìle - TETELESTAI Marital delay - TETELESTAI Power of death - TETELESTAI

Ògwùgo, ògwùgo, ògwùgo - TETELESTAI Ògwùgo, ògwùgo, ògwùgo - TETELESTAI

IT IS FINISHED! TETELESTAI IT IS FINISHED! TETELESTAI

End of the story - TETELESTAI

In the midst of the darkest storms of my life, these songs were my lighthouse. They were the roses that bloomed defiantly in the barren wilderness of my trials. They were evidence that truly one can bloom in a desert.

It's often remarked that one's faith is most severely tested when the tides are against them. Indeed, I had always heard it said that when your faith feels strongest, that's when it comes under the fiercest attack. It's an adage that, until my trials, I had understood only in theory. Now, it was my lived reality.

Faith in the Desert

Imagine for a moment: you're at a point where every material comfort, every piece of your identity, is stripped away. The clothes you wear, the shoes that once danced to life's rhythm, the shelter of a home, the validation of a job, and even the educational certificates that you earned after years of hard work are all gone. The weight of such loss can be soul-crushing, making it almost impossible to hold on to faith. But isn't that when faith matters the most?

There's a profound truth in the biblical passage from Romans 10:17: 'Faith comes by hearing, and hearing by the word of God.' During my desolation, the scriptures became my refuge. The words of Hebrews 11:1, 'Now faith is the assurance of things hoped for, the conviction of things not seen,' became a mantra. Though my reflection showed a frail woman, my spirit clung to a hope anchored in faith.

The bafflement on the face of my studio engineer remains vivid in my mind. Receiving radiotherapy one day and standing in a recording studio the next, belting out songs of hope, was nothing short of a miracle. He'd seen others on the same journey, and they weren't standing, let alone singing. Yet, Mark 9:23 resonated: 'If you can believe, all things are possible to him who believes.'

In the arid desert of trials, faith was my oasis. Ephesians 2:8-9 reminded me, 'For by grace you have been saved through faith, and that not of yourselves; it is the gift of God, not of works, lest anyone should boast.' Even when my strength waned, a mustard seed of faith propelled me forward.

The stories of biblical figures like Sarah bolstered my spirits. Despite being past the age of childbearing, her unwavering faith bore fruit. I, too, held on to the promise that my faith, though tested in the crucible of pain, would see me through.

Blooming Like a Flower

My life has been like a flower trying to bloom in the harshest of deserts. Where most saw only barrenness and despair, I discovered an inner reservoir of strength and hope. And just when it seemed the world had drained me of all vitality, against all odds, I blossomed, radiating resilience and beauty amidst life's arid challenges.

Like rare blooms in the arid desert, I've written twenty-five songs, each chronicling a part of my journey. All twenty-five songs are recorded, and some are released and available on all streaming platforms. The name of one of these songs is the same as the subtitle of this book, underscoring the deep connection between my music and written stories. The vision is for this song to resonate alongside the book's release, offering a harmonious accompaniment to the book. The lyrics are at the end of this book.

Recently, the idea of adapting my journey into a Christian movie or perhaps a series has taken root. Just yesterday, I found myself discussing this possibility. These artistic endeavours, these growing dreams, were once beyond my imagination during my days in what I now term 'Egypt'. Back then, I felt accomplished, but looking back, that version of me seems so limited compared to the person I've become and where I see myself going.

This journey through the wilderness has been about uncovering myself and blooming. While I thought I had a grasp on who I was, this desert phase has revealed hidden depths and talents. It's as if the desert winds have unveiled treasures buried within me. Crafting songs, recording music, and writing a book aren't just milestones; they're glimpses into a self I'm still discovering. And as I reflect, I recognise that Egypt was just the beginning, with so much more of the story left to unfold.

Prayers in the Hospital

I remember one day when I was in the hospital. I was in my little room, and I started to sing. I was singing just for myself, but then I heard someone crying from the next room over. I thought maybe I was bothering them, so I stopped. But the crying continued. It got louder, and then the person from the next room came to see me. She was really upset and told me to keep singing. She said that my singing made her feel better.

The lady was from Jamaica, and she told me she'd been having a hard time. She had been in the hospital for weeks and didn't want to go home. She said she had been mean to the nurses and didn't talk to anyone. She felt alone. She said she had no family or friends to talk to. She told me she felt like she was a mess because she had been smoking marijuana for a long time.

She asked me to help her say sorry to the nurses. So we went together, and she apologised to all of them. After that, we talked more, and I told her about my faith. She said she had never been to church and knew nothing about it. But she wanted to learn. So I prayed with her and even got her a Bible.

There was another lady in the hospital, too, and I prayed with her as well. I felt like this was why I was in the hospital—to help these people. I felt like maybe this was why I was there: to share my faith and help others. We became friends, and I still talk to them. I bought them bibles, and we keep in touch. This experience made me realise that even in hard times, like being in the hospital, good things can happen. It was a turning point for me. You can bloom in the desert. You can be a light in a dark place.

Prophetic Word from Strangers

On another hospital visit, a nurse approached me. As she began to take a blood sample and set up the cannula, she suddenly held my hand and started speaking in tongues. I looked at her in astonishment. This wasn't typical behaviour for a nurse in A&E.

She looked at me with intensity, goosebumps evident on her skin, and said, 'Woman of God, I see something powerful in you. God has big plans for you.' I nodded, replying, 'Yes, I know.'

She continued, 'With your voice, you will reach the world.' I was taken aback. How could this nurse, a stranger, know so much about me? She confessed, 'I don't normally do this. It's not allowed. But something compelled me today.'

The strangest thing, however, was that as soon as I met this nurse, I felt the fever receding. By the time the doctor arrived to discuss admitting me, I confidently questioned, 'Admit me for what? The fever is gone.' I was admitted as they wanted to check everything. The power of that unexpected interaction in the hospital was undeniable and was evidence that God could bring light to the desert.

During one of my routine outings, I had a particularly memorable encounter with an Uber driver. As we journeyed, my nephew tried to sit on my lap. Gently, I explained to him I had recently undergone surgery and couldn't accommodate him there. The driver, overhearing our conversation, expressed his concern, and then, out of the blue, he shared an insight. He said, 'I have this strong intuition that one day you're going to speak, and the whole world will listen.' I was taken aback. I asked him to repeat what he'd just said, not just out of disbelief, but also because the weight of his words resonated deeply with me.

As we continued our conversation, he urged me to look at him. He showed me the goosebumps on his arms, affirming the depth of what he felt. 'I don't know you,' he reiterated, 'but this is what my spirit is telling me.' To my surprise, instead of continuing with his rides for the day, he paused his app to extend our conversation. We found ourselves delving into faith, and he even started discussing passages from his Bible. I was both astonished and heartened to find such a profound connection and wisdom from such an unexpected source.

I recall the story about my young nephew, who was only five years old at the time. After undergoing chemotherapy, my appearance drastically changed, and I was anxious about how he'd react. I didn't look like the auntie he once knew. However, rather than being frightened or distant, he lovingly began to refer to me as 'queen'. It was such a touching gesture. And, to this day, he still calls me by that affectionate title. This, for me, is always a prophetic word from the mouth of a child.

There was a funny occurrence of him calling me this title on the day King Charles III was installed. His mother had called him and told him there was an installation going on, and as the crown was to be placed on his head, he called me, 'Queen, come!' As the crowning was happening on television, his mother excitedly called to him, saying, 'They are crowning the king!' To this, he responded, 'I have crowned the queen!' It was a hilarious occurrence, but a core memory for me, and most especially, a prophetic word.

How to Blossom in the Desert

As we journey through the pages of life, there are inevitable moments that feel barren, much like a desert. These phases, although challenging, are crucial to our personal growth and development. They test our resilience, shape our character, and often set the stage for our most significant transformations. Just as a flower bravely pushes through the arid desert soil to bask in the sun's glory, so, too, can we find our moments to shine amidst adversity. The desert phase might be long, and at times, it may seem endless. But remember, it's in the harshest conditions that nature crafts its most splendid miracles. If you find yourself in such a desert, yearning to bloom, consider these steps as a guiding light:

1. **Embrace the Silence:** The desert may feel lonely and vast, but it's in the quiet moments that we often hear the most. Use this time to meditate, pray, or simply be still. Listen to what the Lord is trying to tell you.
2. **Nourish Your Roots:** Just as a flower needs strong roots to bloom in harsh conditions, you need to nourish your soul and body. Seek out knowledge, read the Bible, and maintain a balanced diet and exercise routine. Your physical and mental well-being are interconnected.

3. **Seek Support:** Even in a desert, life thrives in clusters. Connect with like-minded individuals or groups that can offer guidance, share experiences, or simply listen. Remember, shared burdens often feel lighter.

4. **Celebrate Small Wins:** Every step forward, no matter how tiny, is progress. Did you learn something new? Overcome a personal fear? Or simply get through a tough day? Celebrate it. These minor victories accumulate and pave the way for bigger achievements.

5. **Stay Hopeful and Patient:** Every desert has an oasis, and every winter is followed by spring. Believe that your time to bloom is coming, and remain patient. Your perseverance will be rewarded.

AFFIRMATIONS:

1. I'm chosen, holy, and dearly loved by God.
2. God directs my steps and makes my paths straight.
3. I'm engraved on the palms of God's hands.

Chapter 8

God of Second Chance

The surgeries, the diagnosis, the entire desert experience—they've been a rollercoaster. But if there's anything I've learnt from this tumultuous ride, it is that God is a God of second chances.

One day, I awoke with a clear directive from God. He instructed me to seek seven expectant mothers and offer them blessings. This task involved purchasing gifts for their unborn children. At the time, the reason behind this divine request was unclear to me, yet I did not question it.

I began my search for pregnant women and eventually arrived at a health centre on an antenatal day. There, I contacted a merchant who specialises in importing baby goods from the United Kingdom, ensuring that I acquired high-quality items for the babies. Notably, my actions were not motivated by a personal desire for a child; I was simply fulfilling the task set by God.

Upon my visit to the health centre on the designated day, the matron informed me that exactly seven pregnant women were present. Feeling grateful, I approached these women, knelt before them, and explained my purpose: I had brought gifts for their unborn children and requested their prayers in return. My actions were driven solely by obedience to God's instruction, not by any personal aspiration.

As I knelt there, the women were moved to tears and began to bless and pray for me. They mistakenly believed that my gesture was driven by a longing for a child of my own—which is not so. After this heartfelt exchange, I departed, still unaware of the deeper significance or the future implications of this divinely inspired instruction.

Fibroid Surgery and Complications

After my act of obedience, a dramatic turn of events unfolded a week later. On December 11th, 2020, I underwent fibroid surgery. Initially, it appeared successful, and I was conscious as I was wheeled out of the theatre. However, the following day, my condition drastically worsened. The night before, my prayer leader by the name of Brother Nick visited me in the middle of the night. I was asleep when he did, and this story was relayed to me by my sister. According to Brother Nick, he was asleep when the Lord woke him up and instructed him to come anoint me in the hospital. It was so late that he was scared to drive, so he called someone with a bike, who brought him to the hospital.

Upon arrival, he went straight to my bed and anointed my hands, feet, and head with the words, 'They will be allowed to torture your flesh, but you will not die'. It was the next day, when my condition worsened, that I understood why that was done.

I began experiencing severe, excruciating stomach pain that was beyond explanation. The agony was so intense that I found myself writhing and crying out in pain, even with my stitches. In my distress, I started proclaiming to everyone, including my sister, that I was dying. I lamented how I had walked into the hospital on my own but was now being carried out, seemingly at death's door.

The medical team was baffled. The nurses and doctors were at a loss because, as far as they were concerned, the surgery had been a success. The situation took a grave turn when I started vomiting. It wasn't normal; I was vomiting what appeared to be green bile, and even the catheter had turned green. This alarming development prompted the surgeon to consult with the hospital's managing director and call in a specialist.

When the specialist arrived and saw my condition—with yellowing eyes and pale lips—he immediately instructed the doctor to ensure I didn't die in their facility. They quickly arranged for an ambulance to transfer me out. By this time, my physical strength was ebbing away, and I felt utterly exhausted. I expressed to my sister my readiness to let go and rest.

I was then referred to the Federal Medical Centre (FMC) in Lagos. However, upon arrival, FMC deemed my case beyond their capacity and rejected me. We then moved to a military hospital, but they, too, were hesitant to take me in. Despite my physical weakness, my spirit remained resilient. In my mind, I kept reciting, 'I know my Redeemer lives.'

At the military hospital, the doctors informed my younger sister that I had barely an hour left to live. The situation was dire, but amidst it all, my faith and inner strength continued to resonate within me.

Divine Intervention

The medical staff informed my sister that our options were limited: either take me home or attempt to seek help at Lagos University Teaching Hospital (LUTH). In the ambulance, accompanied by my prayer leader, a significant moment occurred. He shared he had prayed fervently and received a divine assurance that although my body may be afflicted, I would not succumb to this crisis. He said that 'they will torture her flesh, but she will not die.'

Upon reaching LUTH, we were confronted with a dire situation. The emergency ward was overflowing, with no available space. I witnessed people being turned away, some relinquishing hope due to the lack of room. A nurse, observing my critical condition, remarked sceptically about why I was brought there in such a state.

Despite this, my prayer leader remained steadfast in his belief, continually affirming that God had assured him of my survival. He even prayed for guidance to find a specific nurse from LUTH who was part of our prayer group, though he did not have her contact details.

Remarkably, as we arrived at LUTH, it was this very nurse who greeted us at the emergency ward. Initially, she expressed doubt, stating the same issue of overcrowding and advising us to take me home. However, my prayer leader persisted, reiterating the divine message that I would not die.

In a turn of events that can only be described as miraculous, this nurse, who initially suggested sending me home, found a way to admit me. She transformed from someone urging others to turn me away into an advocate, urgently summoning doctors and medical staff, pleading for their assistance, and referring to me as her sister. Her actions and the sudden shift in her stance were nothing short of extraordinary, and I found myself receiving the much-needed medical attention in LUTH against all odds.

Laparotomy and Bowel Resection Surgery

While in the hospital, my condition worsened dramatically. My intestine had ruptured, leading to a horrendous experience where I began to vomit and expel faeces. The medical team had to urgently suction the waste from my nose, mouth, and down into my intestine. This procedure, albeit distressing, was crucial in keeping me alive for the time being.

After enduring this ordeal for some hours, I was eventually

wheeled into a ward. Surgeons soon arrived to prepare me for emergency surgery. At this point, my condition was dire; I was estimated to be 80% deceased.

Amidst this life-threatening situation, my thoughts kept returning to the seven unborn babies I had blessed. I implored them to pray for me, clinging to any semblance of hope.

The medical team explained the gravity of my condition. My intestines had not only ruptured, but I was also suffering from severe sepsis, which had compromised my organs. They proposed a complex surgical procedure called a laparotomy and bowel resection, which would involve removing my entire small intestine, excising the damaged parts, and then stitching it back together. Additionally, they planned to cleanse my liver and kidneys, provided they were still functional.

The doctors were candid about the risks: only one in twenty patients survives such a procedure, and even if I did, I could potentially succumb within 72 hours due to lung failure.

Faced with this daunting prognosis, they asked if I wished to proceed with the surgery. I was also given the opportunity to speak with my family, which felt akin to a final goodbye. My sister, a medical doctor, encouraged me with words of faith and strength, urging me to fight and return. As I was being wheeled into the operating theatre, my mind was fixated on the seven unborn children I had earlier blessed. I silently called out to them, asking for their prayers and intervention. The surgery commenced on the night of December 14th and lasted approximately six hours, ending in the early hours of the morning.

Post-surgery, I was transferred directly to the ICU. The medical team and my loved ones anxiously counted the minutes, bracing for the possibility that my lungs might fail and I might not survive. This period was one of intense uncertainty, with everyone prepared for the worst.

Remarkably, the day after my surgery, I regained consciousness and immediately asked for the life support to be removed so I could breathe on my own. The medical team closely monitored my condition, but it seemed that Jesus had already completed His work. There was a sense of awe in watching over someone whom Jesus had saved.

Two days later, I was wheeled into my room, marking a significant milestone in my recovery. Prior to this, I had undergone two major surgeries, so my return to the room was met with jubilation by the medical staff. However, there was still a palpable sense of apprehension, as everyone was waiting for the critical 72-hour period to pass—it was a period of cautious optimism.

My family, too, endured this anxious wait. As each day passed—the third, fourth, fifth, and sixth days—I remained alive and breathing, defying the grave prognosis. By the seventh day, it was clear that I was not only surviving but also recovering.

Yet, on the eighth day, it felt as though adversity struck again. It seemed as if the devil, seeing my survival, was determined to challenge my life once more. The journey of my recovery was far from over, marked by both miraculous resilience and new trials.

Deep Vein Thrombosis

As I was still in hospital, I was suddenly struck by a condition known as deep vein thrombosis (DVT), where one of my legs became abnormally heavy, weighing around 37 kg. Unfortunately, I didn't initially recognise the seriousness of the issue associated with DVT. With DVT, it's crucial not to touch or manipulate the affected area because disturbing blood clots can lead them to travel to the heart or lungs, potentially causing severe complications or even death.

Now, when DVT struck me, I didn't understand what was happening, and my sister, who had come to visit me in the hospital, started massaging my leg with shea butter, not knowing it was a DVT. My veins were visibly protruding, and she was trying to help by massaging the leg. Little did we know that touching it was the wrong thing to do.

Eventually, one doctor noticed the extreme pain and swelling in my leg. He spoke to my sister and suggested that she should go home to be with her kids since I had been in the hospital for over a week. My sister refused to leave, as she was deeply concerned about my condition.

The doctors understood the severity of my case and believed it was almost a lost cause, given how advanced the DVT was. They tried persuading my sister to leave, as she was getting overwhelmed by the situation.

My sister, however, adamantly refused to leave my side. As the night progressed, something bizarre occurred. She woke up the next morning with large, painful boils on both of her legs. Due to her fair complexion, these boils appeared red. She attempted to stand, but couldn't lift her legs. Her legs were in excruciating pain, and the boils were massive.

Panicked, she called for a doctor to examine her condition. Both her legs had developed these alarming boils within a span of just 24 hours. It was perplexing because we were in a private room at the hospital, which was considered clean and well-maintained. So, there was no apparent source for this sudden affliction. As my sister's condition worsened rapidly, a visitor who had been staying with me advised her to seek treatment from her own doctor. Her legs were deteriorating rapidly, and it was clear that something was terribly wrong.

In the meantime, my sister had become my pillar of strength. I promised her I wouldn't leave her side, and she begged me not to abandon her. I drew strength from her presence and her determination to stay by my side, even when the doctors seemed to have given up on me. The situation took a dark turn when the doctors wanted to separate my sister from me, likely because they believed that my condition was beyond recovery. However, my sister staunchly refused to leave, willing to stay with me, no matter the outcome.

As her health took a sudden, alarming plunge, we turned to prayer and antibiotics. We anointed her feet and fervently prayed for her healing. Despite the dire prognosis, we believed that she would pull through. In a surprising turn of events, a brother in Christ, Brother Nick, prayed for her, and miraculously, the boils began to dry up the next day.

This ordeal was a spiritual battle, as if someone had declared that I had to die and anyone who stood in the way would face dire consequences. Nevertheless, we persisted in our faith and prayers, and eventually, the tide turned in our favour, and my sister and I began to recover.

Miraculous Recovery

While I was in the hospital, the doctors checked on me every five minutes to see if I was still alive. Miraculously, I remained alive, a testament to God's protection. My medical team was extensive and included the lead surgeon, a haematologist, a cardiologist, a biochemist, and a physiotherapist, among others. All these specialists were involved in my care.

At one point, all eight doctors gathered, and one of them, the lead surgeon who had performed the laparotomy and bowel resection, expressed his astonishment at my recovery. He proclaimed I was out of danger and suggested changing my name to 'Miracle,' reflecting the extraordinary nature of my survival.

Despite my critical condition, which had led to a significant weight loss of about 30 kg and a period of 19 days without food or water, I somehow managed to stay alive. I had received eleven pints of blood during this time. My Christmas and New Year were spent in LUTH hospital, but I remained resilient.

A breakthrough occurred when the medical team decided to try feeding me. To everyone's surprise, my system accepted the food, and I was able to digest it properly. My subsequent visit to the toilet was another astonishing milestone, leaving the doctors in disbelief. One of them declared my recovery a success story, something he had never witnessed before. He was adamant about sharing my story, confessing that he couldn't take credit for the surgery's success and couldn't comprehend how I had pulled through. They described the surgery as deadly, yet, against all odds, I was fine.

The doctors ran every possible test to confirm my recovery. Each test result that came back only added to the amazement at my miraculous recovery. This journey, marked by critical surgeries and life-threatening challenges, had become a story of incredible survival and healing.

As I write today, I am a living testament to the fact that God is truly the God of second chances. To many, my story may seem like a journey back from the dead. It is a story I eagerly share, not just to marvel at the miracle but to ignite hope in hearts that may be faltering in the face of despair.

My journey was akin to walking on the edge of a precipice, wavering between life and death. The medical verdict was grim—I was given barely an hour to live. This was not just a prediction; it was a looming reality. But in that critical hour, in what seemed like the final moments of my earthly existence, Jesus intervened.

The message of my testimony is clear and powerful: when all seems lost, when the hour is at its darkest, there is *'Light Through the Dark Desert'*, a divine light that can pierce through the most overwhelming despair. Jesus doesn't just appear at the eleventh hour; He is there even at the zero hour, when hope seems extinct.

LUTH hospital had given me a prognosis of 72 hours post-surgery—a window they believed would mark the end of my life. But in those 72 hours, Jesus made a profound declaration: He had the final say. His message was unequivocal: my flesh could be touched, but my spirit was under His protection. 'This one will not be taken,' He declared.

My story is not just a personal narrative; it's a testimony to a higher purpose. It raises a pivotal question that I now ask God every day: 'What do you want me to do for you?' This question has become my anthem, a guiding light in my continued journey.

I share this testimony not just to recount a miraculous incident, but to offer it as a beacon of hope to anyone who might be on the brink of losing faith. If you find yourself in a situation where all seems lost, remember there is someone up there—Jesus—who can turn the impossible into a living miracle. Just like He did for me.

Life Is Empty Without Jesus

While I was in hospital, my sister handed me my handbag, an elegant Gucci piece I had treasured, saying, 'Look what I found in your wardrobe.' Cradling the bag in my hands, memories of how much I had saved and sacrificed to own this luxury flashed before me. Yet, in the starkness of the hospital room, its glamour seemed unimportant.

Similarly, I was handed my two phones, my lifelines, to the outside world. One had crashed, but the other, still functional, lit up with countless missed notifications. Holding the device, I realised that for three long weeks, I hadn't even given it a thought. Such a vital part of my daily life, and yet, in the grand scheme of things, its absence hadn't made a dent in my existence.

With a sigh, I looked up at my sister, the weight of a newfound realisation heavy on my heart. 'Do you see this?' I asked, gesturing to the bag and phones. 'I spent weeks without them, and I was perfectly fine. All these things we value, we chase after . . . they're not what truly matters.'

My voice grew soft and introspective. 'This experience, this hospital stay, it's shown me just how empty life can be without what's truly important.' I paused, taking a moment to gather my emotions. 'The only constant, the only thing that truly mattered during my time here, was Jesus.'

From Vanity to Virtue

I remember every morning, hours before work, I would sit in front of the mirror, meticulously applying layers of makeup. It wasn't just about looking good; it was a mask I believed I couldn't live without. I remember a colleague once remarking after I had stopped wearing makeup, 'This is the real you. You're beautiful and smart. You never needed that makeup.' It made me reflect. I had been so engrossed in materialism that I had lost touch with my authentic self and, more importantly, with God. Sundays at church were less about worship and more about scouting the latest fashion trends. I'd strategically sit to have the best view of the congregation, noting down styles to replicate later.

This obsession was more than just a vanity project; it was a financial drain. Despite closets full of unworn clothes from shopping sprees in the United States and United Kingdom, I'd often felt like I had nothing to wear. This cycle of endless buying was emptying my wallet and soul. When it came to investing in my spiritual growth, I hesitated. It was clear that my priorities were misplaced.

But life has a way of teaching us. Challenges I faced, like misunderstandings with loved ones, reminded me of the fleeting nature of material things. Harsh words from a brother made me realise that seeking validation from the outside world was a never-ending, unsatisfying quest.

Today, my focus has shifted. I invest in my soul's nourishment. Books that edify my spirit have replaced the endless stream of clothes and shoes. Through trials, I've learnt the true meaning of endurance and resilience. Even in the darkest times, I've found a glimmer of hope, a light in the desert. This journey has taught me to value the intangible, to seek deeper connections, and to prioritise my relationship with God. For those facing similar challenges, remember that true beauty and worth come from within.

From the Rugged Cross to the Radiant Crown

Life is a series of challenges, with each challenge shaping and refining us. James 1:12 encourages us that there's a cross before the crown. For me, this statement rings profoundly true.

My journey has been marked by moments that felt like carrying a heavy cross. These moments of adversity, much like the wilderness that precedes the Promised Land, test us, mould us, and ultimately prepare us for the crowning moments of our lives.

Many Christians yearn for the crown—the blessings, the prosperity, the moments of triumph. Yet, they're reluctant to bear the cross. They want the rewards without the trials, but life doesn't work that way. There's a reason why the wilderness comes before the Promised Land and why Egypt precedes the crossing of the Red Sea. It's a divine design.

Every challenge I face is my cross, my wilderness. But I don't walk alone; I hold Jesus's hand, trusting that this journey will lead me to my Promised Land, where my crown awaits. It's a celestial race, where we work out our salvation with reverence and patience, according to Philippians 2:12. With each tribulation and humiliation, my cross becomes more evident, yet my focus remains on Jesus, the pioneer and perfecter of our faith. He guides me towards my ultimate goal: the crown.

There's a song about the 'Old Rugged Cross' that always resonates with me. It's a symbol of sacrifice, of the path Jesus walked for our redemption. It's a reminder that our journey isn't meant to be smooth. For ministers to preach only prosperity and blessings without acknowledging the rugged cross is misleading. True prosperity, the kind that lasts, comes after walking the challenging path, after enduring the trials, as mentioned in James 1:2-4.

A colleague once told me that if you haven't faced tribulations, you can't truly guide others. It's through these struggles that we are refined. The rugged cross humbles us, teaches us resilience, and prepares us for the blessings that follow.

This journey, with its cross and crown, teaches humility. It's the old rugged cross that grounds us, reminding us of the sacrifices made for us and the sacrifices we must make. Every step on this path, every challenge faced, is a step closer to the crown, the ultimate reward for our faith and endurance.

As we draw this chapter to a close, it's essential to distil the lessons learnt and the profound truths that have been uncovered. The journey through the wilderness, the endurance of trials, and the lessons from the old rugged cross all lead us back to one foundational Christian principle: humility.

H.U.M.I.L.I.T.Y

Humility is not merely a word but a way of life, a guiding principle that should permeate every action, every decision, and every thought. To better grasp and internalise this concept, let's break down the essence of humility into an acronym:

H - Honouring others above oneself (1 Peter 2:17).
U - Understanding our own limitations and God's greatness

(Isaiah 43:19).

M - Modesty in actions and words (1 Peter 4:3, Ephesians 4:29).

I - Introspection, reflecting on our journey with Christ (1 Peter 1:18-21).

L - Listening more to God's voice than worldly distractions (Psalms 46:10).

I - Ignoring the need for earthly accolades and seeking heavenly rewards (Matthew 6:19-21).

T - Trusting God, even in the wilderness (John 14:1).

Y - Yielding to the Lordship of Jesus Christ (James 4:7).

May this acronym serve as a reminder and guidepost in your spiritual journey. As you walk your path, remember that true greatness in God's kingdom stems from a heart full of HUMILITY.

AFFIRMATIONS:

1. I shall not die but live to declare the goodness of God in the land of the living.
2. The Lord fights my battles, and I hold my peace.
3. I'm valued greatly by God.

Chapter 9

Answering When God Calls

There's a voice that's been following me, a gentle tug that's been pulling at the fringes of my soul. It's as if amidst the noise of life, there's a quiet beckoning, a call meant only for my ears. This isn't just about destiny or fate; it's deeper, more profound. It's the sensation of being chosen for a purpose that's greater than anything I've ever imagined.

Every scar I've earned, every tear I've shed, seems to be a chapter of a story that's still unfolding. A story where I'm not just a character, but the protagonist, navigating through plot twists I never saw coming. Like that harrowing episode at sixteen when death's shadow almost claimed me. Or the time I was inexplicably shifted from one hospital to another, only to find myself in a church, under the watchful eyes of a priest who seemed to know more about my destiny than I did.

He said they were after my voice, my star, the very light within me. It was as if there were forces, both dark and divine, battling over my fate. The darkness was trying to extinguish my light, while the divine was moulding me, preparing me for a mission that only I could accomplish.

These experiences weren't mere coincidences; they were clear calls. Signals from the universe that there was a unique path with my name etched onto it. A journey that I was predestined to walk, with trials meant to strengthen me and victories destined to define me.

With every arrow that came my way, every challenge that sought to derail me, there was an underlying message: God was calling. And it wasn't a general summons. It was personal, intimate. A call to step into the light, embrace my destiny, and become the person I was always meant to be.

Attacks on Destiny

One evening, I experienced a deeply unsettling dream in which I was being pursued by malicious men who chased me into my father's room and assaulted me there. The assault occurred in my father's room, and within the dream, I was left bleeding. Upon waking around 2 a.m., to my horror, I discovered I was actually bleeding in reality. Overwhelmed with emotions, I cried, feeling utterly besieged by these attacks, and even questioned God's protection, particularly after the reassurances I had felt from a verse in Isaiah 44, which I had read earlier that night.

The stomach pain that ensued was unbearable, leaving me writhing on the floor in agony, alone in my room while working offshore. After a struggle, I managed to clean myself up, and then, exhausted, I returned to bed. Before falling asleep again, I pleaded with God for a way out of my suffering.

That same night, I had another dream. This time, I found myself at a church programme led by Bishop David Oyedepo—The Living Faith Church, AKA Winners Chapel. Although I wasn't a member of that church and had no particular affinity for it, I was there in the dream, feeling dirty and repulsive, causing me to retreat further back from the congregation. Unexpectedly, Bishop

Oyedepo and his wife noticed me from the pulpit and approached me, even as I tried to run away. When he laid his hands on me, a bird flew out from my head, my filthy clothes turned white, and those who had previously recoiled began to admire me, including celebrities and notable people. These people began to tell me how beautiful I was. They led me to the pulpit, where I began to prophesy.

Upon waking at 5 a.m., my hand brushed against a flyer on the floor, a flyer for Shiloh 2010, an event organised by Winners Chapel, which I had no prior intention of attending. Yet the flyer featured the same man of God and his wife, who had appeared in my dream. This synchronicity convinced me I needed to attend that programme. Fortunately, I was due to leave the offshore site the day before Shiloh began.

Upon returning home, I discovered my neighbour was their church member and planned to attend. However, when he unexpectedly did not return the next day, I didn't hesitate; I took a cab and then a motorbike due to the traffic, determined to reach Canaan Land for the event.

The Shiloh programme was vast, with countless attendees onsite and more participating online. My plans were disrupted multiple times, and during my stay, I developed a painful skin condition. But I was determined to stay, believing that this place would bring me healing.

Despite advice to leave and seek medical attention, I chose to stay, putting my faith first. Miraculously, by the end of the event, my skin cleared up, and I left feeling both physically and spiritually restored.

This experience taught me a powerful lesson: when you're marked by destiny, adversarial forces will always mount their challenge. But with steadfast faith, these challenges can be faced and overcome, allowing one to fully embrace their divine calling.

This dream later manifested in reality, where I met Bishop Oyedepo and received blessings, including an anointing oil. Such meetings were effortless for me, while others yearned for a mere glimpse.

The Giant Snake

In a vivid dream, I found myself at my father's house. From the kitchen, a small snake appeared. But as I watched, it grew taller and bigger into a giant snake, its head nearly touching the clouds.

The giant snake spoke to me, angry and accusing. It claimed that the house, the land, had always been its territory. We argued, but then I switched tactics. Instead of words, I began speaking in a spiritual tongue.

As I did, the snake retreated, although it tried to fight back by throwing fiery venom at me. When it was nearly driven away, it cried, upset about being forced out.

Waking up, I shared my dream with my pastor. She said it symbolised old challenges and enemies trying to stop me from my life's purpose. Just as the serpent in Eden sought to alter destiny, the devil will always aim to abort the destinies of those with a higher calling. But with faith, strength, and spiritual resilience, we can prevail.

Divine Surrender

Throughout my life, I've felt the tug of divine direction urging me to surrender control and hand over the reins of my existence to God. But, like many, I wrestled with this call. The struggle was real, a tug-of-war between my earthly desires and God's heavenly purpose for me.

So, what does surrender truly entail?

For me, surrender is a process of emptying oneself and making room for the Divine. It means letting go of ego, personal desires, and earthly concerns and allowing God to infuse us with His spirit. It's a journey from 'me' to 'He'. A shift from worldly desires to spiritual aspirations.

It's an 'Abrahamic process'—a reference to the biblical Abraham, who was willing to sacrifice his son Isaac in obedience to God, exemplifying ultimate surrender and trust in God's plan. It might seem irrational to the world, but in the eyes of faith, it's the wisest decision one can make.

In surrendering, we're not giving up, but rather embracing a deeper trust. Trusting that the One who beckons us to this path has a grand design, a purpose that far exceeds our understanding. It's a journey into the unexpected, anchored in unwavering faith.

In essence, total surrender is not about losing oneself, but about finding oneself in God. It's a leap of faith, trusting that He will catch you, guide you, and lead you to the destiny He's crafted just for you.

Once I truly surrendered, the transformation was palpable. There was an overwhelming sense of peace and joy that's difficult to describe. Even in moments of external chaos or sadness, my heart danced in praise and worship. Instead of being driven by fear, my actions were driven by faith. There was a renewed closeness with God, a hunger for His presence, and a resilience that was previously absent.

Living a Life of Surrender

Maintaining a surrendered heart is about daily choices. It means immersing oneself in God's Word, staying connected through prayer, and being attuned to His voice in every situation. When challenges arise, instead of succumbing to them, I feel God's reassuring presence lifting and guiding me.

To anyone on the fence about surrendering, I'd say: take the plunge! The peace, joy, and purpose you'll find in Christ far outweigh any worldly concerns. Without Jesus, life feels like a series of crises. True riches aren't about material wealth, but spiritual abundance. Spiritual poverty, being distant from God, is the real tragedy. Embrace Christ, and you'll truly understand the goodness and reality of God.

Divine Placement

Divine placement is essentially the idea of being at the right place at the right time for a greater purpose, often to be a part of someone's salvation or a miracle. This concept speaks to the divine orchestration of events and circumstances to align with God's will for an individual or a situation.

Many individuals miss out on reaching their God-ordained

destinies due to a lack of spiritual foresight or divine guidance. A vivid example is spending years in a certain job, like with Chevron, feeling unfulfilled and constantly struggling. While for some, being in such a renowned company might seem like the pinnacle of success, for others, it could be a source of unending dissatisfaction.

Being in the right place at the wrong time or vice versa can lead to profound feelings of frustration and stagnation. It's a poignant reminder that while a place or situation might be perfect for one person, it could be entirely wrong for another. Just because circumstances align for someone else doesn't mean they will for you if you're not where you're divinely meant to be.

There are times when this misalignment can lead to feelings of anger and frustration towards God, especially when one believes they've followed divine guidance faithfully. It's an agonising experience to watch others progress and achieve their goals while feeling stuck in a cycle of stagnancy.

However, understanding the concept of divine placement can provide clarity. It's not about being in a renowned place or situation, but being where God wants you to be. When you're in the place God has ordained for you, things start to align, and you find purpose and fulfilment.

The Timing of God

God will never allow you to get to the place where you are meant to be before you are well-prepared or ready for what He has for you. God's timing is impeccable. He will only place you in your destined role once you are sufficiently equipped for the challenges it holds. He might illuminate your path, even give glimpses of your destiny, but until you've undergone His refining process, you won't step into your true calling. Each trial and lesson you face is foundational for your divine assignment.

God gave me another dream where I recall vividly my encounter with Pastor Enoch Adeboye—the general overseer of the Redeemed Christian Church of God.

When he and I embarked on a journey together, our destination was unclear to me, but I knew we were set to harvest something. The terrain was challenging, strewn with rocks and hills, and during our travel, we noticed people scurrying back to their homes in panic due to an approaching tempest. Despite the chaos and the thickening clouds, as people fled from the oncoming storm, shouting in fear, Pastor Adeboye remained undeterred. He grasped my hand firmly, indicating we should proceed towards the very scene from which others were escaping.

With determination, he carried a sturdy iron rod typically used for harvesting yams—a staple in our diet. He handed me a knife to assist in the harvest. As we ventured on, the storm loomed closer, but we pressed forward to a deserted farmland that required navigating a hill to reach. This land, which had been abandoned for years, was surprisingly abundant with wheat.

Upon arrival, he declared it was time to begin the harvest. The yams we unearthed from the neglected soil were enormous and beyond anything imaginable. Not a single crop had been planted on this land, yet here we were, reaping vast and plump yams.

Before long, the once barren land was teeming with produce. Astonishingly, people from nearby villages began to converge, seeking sustenance from this once-forsaken place. They were in disbelief, questioning how such a bountiful harvest was possible on land where nothing had been sown.

We shared the harvest generously, and the villagers took it from the land, marvelling at the unexpected blessing. I awoke from the dream on the 25th of July, 2021—a remarkable dream that occurred just ten days after my arrival in the United Kingdom on the 15th of July.

Yet, readiness is essential. Like Joseph in Genesis 37:5-11, who was shown his destiny but not the timeline, we must be patient.

God has reserved a specific moment for each of us, accompanied by divine provisions. However, many remain ignorant of this, clinging to their comfort zones, leading to prolonged struggles.

I, too, fell into the trap of comfort. Despite knowing God was calling me elsewhere, I clung to my job at Chevron out of fear of the unknown. This resistance resulted in nearly a decade of feeling out of place, wasting precious time that could've been spent fulfilling my true purpose. Often, we're so daunted by the journey ahead that we forget God's promises and revert to our familiar 'Egypt', even if it means forgoing our promised 'Canaan'.

The challenge is to push beyond our comfort zones, trusting in God's plan and His perfect timing, even when the path seems uncertain. By doing so, we align ourselves with His divine purpose and step into the destiny He has ordained for us.

Your Place of Blessing

One of the foundational truths in understanding God's plan for our lives is recognising the importance of being in the right place. God's blessings are often tied to specific places or assignments He has for us. Just being somewhere at the 'right time' doesn't necessarily mean it's the right place for you.

Consider the analogy of being 'at the right place but at the wrong time', or vice versa. While these phrases might sound puzzling, they underscore a vital truth: just because a situation seems right doesn't mean it's God's ordained place or time for you. Something happened to me recently that reinforced this revelation. Because of my illness and the challenges that came with it, I found myself in between jobs and trying to make ends meet. I kept praying for God to make a way, and then, one day, I got a call to interview for a job. The job was very flexible and was going to cater to my accommodation. With rent and bills out of the way, I had little to worry about. An answer had come. Finally! Or so I thought. I met the boss and went through an interview with him. Everything was attractive, from the flexibility to the working arrangements. I made up my mind to take up the offer. However, when I got home, I was very unsettled. There was a knot in my belly about the situation and I couldn't figure out what was wrong.

An answer to my prayer had come. It seemed right, so what could be wrong? After a few days of contemplation, I decided to visit again. When I did, I was even more attracted to the role. I kept searching my spirit to understand what was wrong, but nothing specific was highlighted to me. I decided I was going to start the job in two days, as they wanted me to resume as soon as it was possible. Upon getting home, the discomfort returned and so I decided to pray. I had been praying before, but I prayed more intensely and decided to be more receptive to 'Lord, your will' rather than 'Lord, approve this'. That very night, I had two dreams that provided me with some clarity. One in particular was about a brother of mine bringing me light in a dark situation. The following day, I got a call from him offering me a job. As if that was not enough, I got two more calls the same day, with different offers.

Though now I cannot explicitly state what the red light in my spirit was for, I came to know through prayers and revelation through dreams God's will. I understood that, though it seemed right, it was not God's ordained place or time for me to work there. In a similar fashion, the question isn't just if the time or place is right in a general sense, but is it right *for you*?

Reflecting on Abraham's journey can offer deeper insights. God instructed Abraham to leave his familiar surroundings and go to a place He would show him. It was in that designated place that God promised to bless Abraham and make him a great nation. This narrative emphasises that divine blessings are often tied to obedience and being in the place God has destined for you.

For those who are chosen or have a specific call on their lives, this truth becomes even more critical. There's no shortcut to divine blessings. One might venture far and wide, but they'll often find themselves returning to the starting point if they're not in their God-ordained place.

It's essential, especially for those who feel a divine call or assignment, to discern their place in God's kingdom early on. Once you've identified who you are in Christ and the purpose He has for you, it's crucial to align yourself with that purpose. Otherwise, you risk missing out on the blessings God has for you in the place He's prepared.

Finding Your Divine Placement

To truly flourish in life and achieve our God-ordained destinies, it's crucial to be in the right place at the right time, our so-called 'divine placement'. But how can you discern this perfect positioning?

1. **Recognising Discontent:**
    - Signs you're in the wrong place might be evident. If you're unhappy, especially in situations or places that once brought joy or contentment, it's a red flag.
    - Dissatisfaction with work or a sudden feeling of everything going awry can signal that you're not where you're meant to be.

2. **Inner Peace:**
   - True divine placement brings peace. Even when everything is not perfect, a profound inner calm suggests you're where God intends.
   - Conversely, feeling uncomfortable, even in seemingly comfortable situations, is a sign you might be out of alignment.

3. **Resistance and Challenges:**
   - The journey to your divine placement won't necessarily be easy. Expect resistance, especially from forces like the devil, who might not want you to reach your divinely ordained position.
   - Struggles and challenges on the path can sometimes be affirmations that you're on the right track.

4. **Seasons of Life:**
   - Recognise when a season in your life is over. When things suddenly become uncomfortable, or you feel out of place, it might be time to move to the next chapter God has for you.

5. **Affirmations and Signs:**
   - God often confirms our paths. It might be through dreams, through people, or uncanny real-life situations that seem more than mere coincidences.

- Meeting people you've longed to meet or having doors open in unexpected ways can be confirmations that you're heading in the right direction.

6. **Answering God's Call:**
   - Being in your divine placement often aligns with answering a specific call from God. This is not just about being in the right location or job, but also about fulfilling a higher purpose or mission.
   - Responding to this call often brings an unparalleled sense of peace and purpose, guiding you to your true divine positioning.

In conclusion, finding your divine placement is an intimate journey of obedience, prayer, and discernment. It requires patience, faith, and a keen sensitivity to God's leading. By paying attention to these signs and continually seeking divine guidance, you can navigate your path with confidence, knowing you're walking in the direction God has intended for you.

AFFIRMATIONS:

1. God is my safe place; I go to Him because I trust Him.
2. God has a purpose for my life.
3. I'm more than an overcomer through Christ.

Chapter 10

God's Unconditional Love

It happened during the harrowing days of chemotherapy. The treatments had transformed me into a shadow of my former self. I had grown to dread mirrors, each reflection only amplifying the stark contrast between who I once was and the stranger I now saw. An elderly lady I'd met during one of my treatments had wisely advised, 'Do not look in the mirror, dear. That alone is enough to kill you.'

En route to the hospital for my chemotherapy session, I found myself ensnared by overwhelming sorrow. Tears streamed down my face as the weight of the impending treatment bore down on me. In my anguish, I poured out my heart to God, lamenting my aversion to chemotherapy. In response to my despair, He bestowed upon me a song inspired by Psalm 121, turning my moment of pain into a beacon of hope. The song is ODUM IJE—which means 'My Journey Escort.'

God's Unconditional Love

Verse 1

I lift my eyes to the hill

From whence comest my help

My help comes from the Lord Jesus

He will not suffer

my foot to be moved

My help comes from the Lord Jesus

Chorus:

Odumije, Odumije, Odumije, Odumije

Verse 2

The lord is my keeper

The lord is my shield

Upon my right hand

The sun shall not smite me by day

Nor the moon by night

My help comes from Jesus

He shall preserve my going out and coming in

My help comes from the Lord Jesus

He shall preserve my going out and coming in

My help comes from the Lord Jesus

Odumije, Odumije, Odumije, Odumije

Odumije by Chidimma D. Onuoha

One Sunday, I decided to brave the outside world, seeking solace in a simple walk. On an unusual impulse, I removed my protective face mask, feeling the cool air on my skin for the first time in what felt like forever. As I walked, I was consumed by my thoughts, reflecting on the dramatic changes in my appearance: the puffiness from the steroids, the deep, almost unnatural hue of my skin, and the complete absence of my once-lush hair.

Lost in my contemplation, I found myself sitting at a bus stop. It was there that I noticed a man walking past. I thought little of it until, on my way home, our paths crossed again. As I walked past him, he unexpectedly turned and exclaimed, 'Beautiful lady!'

Shocked, I looked around, unable to believe he was referring to me. 'I'm talking to you,' he insisted. 'Can I speak with you?'

I was taken aback. Here was a stranger, looking at my hairless, darkened face, devoid of eyebrows and lashes, and still finding beauty. 'Can't you see my face?' I stammered incredulously.

'I've seen your face,' he replied calmly, 'and I see your heart. You are beautiful inside and out.'

That brief encounter was a revelation. At a time when I felt at my lowest, deeming myself the 'ugliest human being in the world', someone saw past the physical changes, the scars, and the pain. They saw a beauty that was not just skin deep, but radiated from within.

I realised then that this was a glimpse of God's unconditional love. Just as that stranger saw beauty in me, despite the outward changes, God sees us for who we truly are. His love is unfaltering, unwavering, and undiscriminating. He loves us regardless of our physical appearance, our flaws, or our past mistakes.

In moments of self-doubt and despair, it's essential to remember this profound love. God's love for us is not contingent on our circumstances, our achievements, or how we perceive ourselves. It is a love that is boundless and all-encompassing.

In life, we all have moments when we feel lost, unloved, or out of place. Yet, it's these moments that often lead to profound realisations and encounters that remind us of the ever-present love of God. For in His eyes, we are always loved, always cherished, and forever beautiful.

The Depths of Divine Love

In the Book of Romans, a profound declaration is made: 'But God demonstrates His own love toward us, in that while we were still sinners, Christ died for us' (Romans 5:8).

This verse encapsulates the essence of God's love for us. His love isn't predicated on our virtues, our deeds, or our religious observances. It's unwavering, steadfast, and unconditional.

It's a concept that can be challenging to grasp, especially during times of hardship and uncertainty. When we're lost in our personal wilderness, battling internal and external demons, it can be easy to question God's love for us. The darkness we sometimes find ourselves in can shroud the omnipresence of His love.

Yet, it's precisely during these wilderness moments that God's love shines the brightest. It becomes our beacon, guiding us through our lowest points and reminding us of our inherent worth in His eyes.

There have been countless moments in my spiritual journey when I've felt unworthy of His love. The burden of sin, the weight of guilt, and the voice of the adversary have often made me question my worthiness. It's in these moments of self-doubt that the enemy tries to distance us from God, making us feel isolated and condemned.

But God's message is clear: He loves us not because of who we are, but *in spite of* who we are. He doesn't see our flaws and shortcomings; He sees our hearts. His love isn't contingent on our righteousness or perfection. He loves us because we are His creations, and that love remains constant, regardless of our actions or beliefs.

In 1 John 4:9-10, we're reminded: 'In this the love of God was manifested toward us, that God has sent His only begotten Son into the world, that we might live through Him. In this is love, not that we loved God, but that He loved us and sent His Son to be the propitiation for our sins.'

This is the epitome of unconditional love. A love that sacrifices, that gives without expecting anything in return, and that sees beyond our human frailties.

John 15:13 further reiterates this message: 'Greater love has no one than this: to lay down one's life for one's friends.'

No matter how far we feel we've strayed, no matter how tarnished we believe our souls have become, God's love remains. His love isn't a reward for our righteousness; it's a gift freely given, reminding us we are cherished, valued, and eternally loved.

God's Love Through People

Life's adversities have a way of testing our faith, making us question our beliefs and the divine plan that's laid out for us. One of the most profound sorrows I've faced was the abandonment I felt, most poignantly, from my own father. This void left me questioning my worth and place in the world, leading me to fervently seek solace in prayer. I remember distinctly asking God why I had to bear this pain and yearning for a father figure in my life. Despite my trials, I've always felt God's omnipresent love surrounding me. His love manifested in myriad ways, often through the kindness of strangers.

One example was during a routine trip to Asda. As I queued to pay for my vegetables, I was approached by an elderly man. Curiously, he inquired about my selection, which consisted mainly of spinach and wild blueberries. Our exchange started off a bit confrontationally, with me questioning his interest in my purchases. However, his good humour prevailed, leading to laughter and a lighthearted conversation. Before I could leave, he generously offered me an assortment of vegetables from his garden, insisting they'd benefit me.

As I made my way to the exit, he called out, asking if he could have my contact details. With a sincere look, he explained his desire to assist me, urging me not to be alarmed. He spoke of his garden, filled with the very produce I was purchasing, and offered them to me freely. His next words were what struck me the most: 'See me as your father.' At a time when I felt utterly abandoned by my own, here was a stranger offering the unconditional love and support I yearned for.

We exchanged numbers, and over time, our bond deepened. He'd call and speak to me as if I were his own, showering me with love and concern. This Greek gentleman, already a father to a daughter in Greece, told her about me, saying she now had a sister. Our bond was epitomised when he took me shopping, insisting on buying me everything I needed. He'd lovingly guide my choices, ensuring I only chose what was best for my health.

Another example of God's love through people and how it was such an extension of heaven in my time of need was the divine meeting I had with a 70+ woman about this same time. I was returning home from a place and was at the train station. She also stood on the platform, poised for the train's arrival. However, when the train came, for some reason, it zoomed right past us and did not pick anyone up. I looked around in shock, and our faces met; she also expressed similar emotions of disappointment, and we got talking. She made a statement about how she believes everything works together for her good, and I found some comfort in that.

Shortly after, the train arrived, and we went aboard together. We continued the conversation, and along the way, she shared something a pastor had shared in the morning. It sounded familiar; she then said, 'What God cannot do . . .' To which I replied, '. . . does not exist!' It then made sense that we both belonged to the same online community of a divine prayer altar by a man of

God, Pastor Jerry Eze. This made us share more and get to know each other. At this time, I had some constraints around the accommodation where I was, and I needed an option for a short while. I had been praying about it, asking God to send me a helper. So, when I met this woman, I pondered whether I should mention this challenge to her, but then, I felt it was not appropriate as we had just met. When we arrived at our destination, I prayed a short prayer, asking the Lord to make our paths cross again if she could do something for my situation.

As I was connecting trains home, I had one more to take. But as I stood there, my phone rang. The call ended up being for about thirty-five minutes, and as I delayed boarding my train, this woman came around the corner again! We connected again, and she invited me to visit her at home. I did and got an opportunity to share my story. I was so surprised when she offered to accommodate me for a bit. It was an answered prayer and gave me the time to recalculate my next moves. She calls me daughter, and I call her mother because that is what she has been to me. She eventually got to meet the Greek gentleman from earlier, and they've both been such an immense blessing to me.

In these moments, I felt God's love shining brightly through this kind-hearted man and woman. I find it interesting that they were advanced in age and now serve as parent figures for me. Despite the hurt of my father's abandonment, God reassured me of His eternal love by placing guardian angels in my path. It's a testament to the fact that God's love often manifests through the kindness of the people around us.

Accepting God's Unconditional Love

If you're wrestling with the idea of God's unconditional and immeasurable love, especially during your darkest moments, consider the following points:

1. **Darkness All Around:** It's only natural when enveloped in darkness to see nothing else but that very darkness. It's not your fault to feel overwhelmed or lost in such moments.
2. **Look for the Light:** Just as this book suggests, even in the darkest desert, there is a glimmer of light. Seek that light, no matter how faint it might seem.
3. **Hold On to Jesus:** Jesus, who gave His life for you, remains a beacon of hope and love. Trust in His love, for it is unwavering and eternal.
4. **Unconditional Love:** Remember, He loved us even when we were sinners. His love isn't based on our righteousness,

but on His boundless mercy and grace.

5. **Dealing with Doubts:** If you ever find yourself questioning God's love for you, recall that nothing can separate you from His love. When the devil tries to sow seeds of doubt, remember that God's love is greater than any sin or shortcoming.

6. **He Qualifies the Called:** God doesn't look for the qualified; He prepares those He calls. He will guide you through your challenges, refining you for His purpose.

7. **A Personal Invitation:** Jesus said, 'Come to me, all who are weary and burdened, and I will give you rest.' Accept His invitation, for He has an abundance of love to share.

8. **Unconditional, No Matter What:** Regardless of how stained or unworthy you might feel, God's love remains steadfast. I've walked this journey feeling undeserving, yet He held me close. Today, I stand as a testimony to His love, sharing my story with the world.

In conclusion, always remember, no matter where you are or what you've done, God's love is ever-present, unwavering, and, most importantly, unconditional. He loves us, always and forever.

AFFIRMATIONS:

1. I'm loved and greatly helped by God.
2. I'm a chosen generation and a royal priesthood, holy and special.
3. I'm a child of God and an heir to His promises.

Chapter 11

Discomfort of the Chosen

The concept of the chosen feeling discomfort in their comfort zones is not new. It is a recurring theme, especially in spiritual journeys. When an individual is destined for a higher purpose, mere comfort often becomes a hindrance. It's God's way of nudging, or sometimes shoving, them towards their true calling.

Take Moses, for instance. Raised as Egyptian royalty, he lived a life of unparalleled luxury and privilege. The palace, with its grandeur, could easily represent the epitome of a 'comfort zone'. Yet, deep down, Moses felt a profound discomfort. It was as if something whispered to him that he was meant for more than the decadent feasts and the echo of laughter in marble halls. His spirit was restless, knowing that beneath the facade of comfort lay his true destiny.

When the moment of revelation arrived, it was not amidst the comforts of the palace but in the stark wilderness, far from the trappings of royalty. The burning bush, a divine paradox of fire that did not consume, was emblematic of Moses's own life. He had been aflame with a purpose he didn't fully comprehend, living in a place that did not diminish his true essence.

Moses's journey from the heart of Egyptian luxury to leading the Israelites through the desert is a testament to the discomfort of the chosen in comfort zones. The palace, for all its allure, was never his destiny. His true calling was amidst the sand dunes and under the vast desert sky, leading his people to freedom.

For many of us, our 'palace' could be a job that pays well but doesn't fulfil our passion. It could be a relationship that's comfortable but not nurturing our growth. Or perhaps a routine that's easy but stifling. The lesson from Moses is clear: sometimes, our very comfort zones, no matter how gilded, can be the chains that keep us from our true destiny.

My Season of Discomfort

In the bustling corridors of Chevron, one of the world's leading oil-producing companies, I often found myself pausing. For many, these halls were the pinnacle of achievement, an emblem of status and ambition fulfilled. Yet, each morning, as I walked through them, an insidious discomfort tugged at me. For a decade, amidst an eighteen-year tenure, this feeling persisted, lurking beneath the surface of accolades and privileges.

Every day, surrounded by the trappings of success and pressures of the industry, I felt like a square peg in a round hole. The prestige of the role, while alluring to others, felt like handcuffs to me. I was achieving, yet not thriving; moving, but not truly growing.

The perks of the job were undeniable. A schedule that allowed me two weeks of work followed by two weeks of leisure, opportunities to travel the globe, and a handsome pay check that promised security. These comforts, however, began to feel more like golden shackles, binding me to a role that didn't resonate with my inner calling.

While the restlessness grew within, a formidable adversary held me in its grip: the fear of the unknown. The vast expanse outside the familiar confines of Chevron was daunting. Would I succeed or falter if I dared to step out?

Physical and mental strain started manifesting as clear indicators of the battle within. Sleepless nights became my constant companion. Each morning, I would find myself confiding in my office neighbour, trying to articulate my feelings of displacement. My reliance on antidepressants and sleeping pills was proof of the toll this internal struggle was taking on me.

Amidst all this, a profound realisation dawned. The awards and recognitions, while gratifying, were not true indicators of personal fulfilment. Training newcomers who would eventually surpass me on the corporate ladder further highlighted this sentiment. The issue wasn't that the job wasn't good; it was simply not right for *me*.

Just as Moses felt out of place amidst the opulence of the Pharaoh's palace, my heart echoed similar sentiments within Chevron's walls. Such chapters in life serve as poignant reminders: societal definitions of success don't always guarantee personal fulfilment. True growth often demands stepping out of our comfort zones, answering the calls of our divine assignments, and journeying into the unknown.

Stepping Into Uncharted Territory

Life often demands that we challenge ourselves, that we step into territories uncharted. With every step outside our comfort zones, we encounter not just the exhilarating thrill of the new, but also the daunting whispers of doubt and trepidation. Here are some of the challenges of breaking free from this comfortable zone:

Standing Alone: One overwhelming feeling I often encountered was the sensation of being out of place, of not conforming to the norm. Even when the majority are drawn in a certain direction by popular trends or opinions, maintaining one's personal beliefs can feel lonely. However, just because you stand alone doesn't mean you're on the wrong path.

Feeling Out of Place: This feeling often dovetails with standing alone. There's a conspicuous sense of being a misfit, especially when you're striding on a path not frequently trodden. The sidelong glances, the unspoken judgements—they all contribute to this feeling.

Abandonment: As you shift away from the crowd, a sense of abandonment can set in. Friends and acquaintances might distance themselves, unsure of how to interact with this 'changed' version of you. They may even regard you with a mix of puzzlement and wariness, making you feel even more isolated.

Fear of the Unknown: One of the most formidable challenges is the fear of what lies ahead. The 'what ifs' can be paralysing, often holding one back from taking the plunge.

Temptation: The allure of the familiar, the siren call of the past, can be tempting. At times, it might feel easier to revert to old ways, to return to the crowd, and forsake one's chosen path.

Spiritual Battles: Faith is often put to the test during these transitions. The devil might sow seeds of doubt, making you question your choices. But as the Bible teaches, faith comes from hearing the message, and the message is heard through the Word about Christ.

In these times of doubt, it's crucial to remember that while the journey might be solitary, you're not truly alone. Seeking guidance, be it through spiritual mentors or personal reflection, can be invaluable. As you navigate these challenges, let your convictions guide you, and remember that growth often comes swathed in discomfort.

Faith Through the Transition

Every leap into the unknown, every step beyond the comfort zone, is an act of faith. Faith isn't just the belief in what we cannot see;

it is also the trust in what we feel and know deep down. For me, faith has been a lifeline, a compass guiding me through the fog of uncertainty.

My faith has been fortified by the simple principle that 'faith comes by hearing, and hearing by the Word of God.' To venture beyond one's comfort zone, a robust faith is nonnegotiable. It's not just about belief; it's about trust. Trust so unwavering that it might make one appear foolish in the eyes of others. But as history has shown, faith's 'foolishness' is often the precursor to profound wisdom.

Consider Abraham, a father of faith. When God instructed him, 'Move from your father's house, from your kindred to a place I have prepared,' Abraham, without hesitation, stepped out. Or when he was asked to sacrifice his son, his obedience was immediate. To the external world, these actions might have appeared irrational, but they stemmed from an unparalleled trust in God.

Such faith can sometimes make us act in ways inconceivable to our past selves. We might be led to places we never imagined or asked to make sacrifices we never thought possible. But it's this very faith that empowers us, ensuring we never walk alone, even when the path is uncharted.

To nurture this faith, I've surrounded myself with the Word

of God. Through books, journals, sermons, and teachings, I've sought to immerse myself in His message. These resources have been my reservoirs of strength, constantly reminding me of His promises and plans for me. Every scripture, every sermon, has been a reaffirmation of His presence and guidance.

In moments of doubt, when the temptation to revert to my comfort zone looms large, it's my faith that anchors me. It reminds me that even if the journey is fraught with challenges, the destination is worth every step. For faith isn't just about believing; it's about surrendering to a higher purpose, a divine plan that far exceeds our own understanding.

And so, as I journey through life's transitions, my faith is my guide, my shield, and my strength. It has not just helped me move beyond my comfort zones, but has also transformed them, turning every challenge into a testament to God's love and grace.

Strategies for Stepping Out of Your Comfort Zone

The journey from the familiar confines of comfort to the unfamiliar terrains of challenge is seldom easy. Over the years, I've found that embracing the discomfort that comes with breaking free of these confines requires not just courage, but also a set of strategies and mindsets.

1. **Immerse in the Word:** Just as I've mentioned earlier, the foundational strategy for me has been studying the Word of God. It offers clarity, direction, and strength. When confronted with doubt or fear, the Word has been my guiding light.

2. **Praising in the Wilderness:** There's immense power in praise. Even in the wilderness, when loneliness looms large, praise can be a beacon. In those moments of solitude, praising God has often brought me comfort and reassurance.

3. **Creative Expression:** Writing songs, penning thoughts, and authoring books have been therapeutic for me. They're not just outlets for my emotions, but also tools to reflect and grow.

4. **Avoid the Noise:** It's crucial to stay away from negativity. Noisy people, those who are excessively talkative without substance or those who spew toxicity, can distract and derail. Surround yourself with positive influences and thoughts.

5. **Reaffirm Your Identity:** Remind yourself daily of your

purpose. I often tell myself, 'I am the light.' Such affirmations can act as anchors, ensuring you don't drift amidst the currents of doubt.

6. **Embrace the Wilderness:** It might sound counterintuitive, but there's value in embracing the discomfort of the wilderness. It's in this wilderness that giants are moulded. It's where you're refined, shaped, and made ready for the platform God has prepared for you.

7. **Seek Mentorship:** It's always beneficial to have spiritual guides or mentors. They can offer counsel, share their experiences, and guide you through the rough patches.

8. **Challenge Your Fears:** Every time you feel afraid or doubt your path, confront those feelings. Ask yourself, 'What's the worst that can happen?' Often, you'll find that your fears are mere shadows, magnified by overthinking.

9. **Celebrate Small Wins:** Every step out of the comfort zone is a victory. Celebrate it. These small celebrations can motivate you to take the next step and the one after that.

10. **Visualise Your Success:** Imagine yourself succeeding, standing on that platform God has prepared for you, sharing your message, and making a difference. This vision can propel you forward.

To anyone feeling the discomfort of being chosen but hesitant to step out of their comfort zone, remember: every great journey begins with a single step. The wilderness might seem daunting, but it's also where legends are born. Embrace it, learn from it, and let it prepare you for the greatness that awaits. Remember, you're not just stepping out; you're stepping up.

AFFIRMATIONS:

1. I don't walk alone; I walk with God the Father, Son, and Holy Spirit.
2. The Spirit of God within me gives me power, love, and a sound mind.
3. I'm remarkably made.

Chapter 12

Shedding Weights in the Wilderness

Growing up, I was captivated by stories of adventure and life lessons, one of which still resonates with me to this day. It's the story of a hunter, a skilled one at that, who ventured into the wilderness and managed to capture two magnificent animals. These creatures, large and bountiful, promised a feast for him and his family, a reward for his prowess.

However, on his triumphant journey back, something unexpected caught his eye—a small, nimble grasshopper. Its movements, perhaps its very essence, enticed him. Even though his hands were full with the weight of his grand catches, the allure of the grasshopper was irresistible. He started pursuing it, trying to capture it with his feet, letting the distraction guide his steps.

Time passed, and the path became unfamiliar. The hunter, engrossed in his pursuit of the minute creature, lost his way. In the blink of an eye, his fortune turned. From being the predator, he became the prey and was devoured by a larger beast. His grand captures, the promise of a feast, were all forsaken for an inconsequential chase.

Isn't that allegory a striking representation of our lives? We often hold on to immense blessings, opportunities, and potential, yet allow minor distractions, grievances, and resentments to divert our course. The 'grasshoppers' in our life—be it bitterness, grudges, or past hurts—may seem trivial, but can lead us astray from our destined path.

These emotional burdens, these 'weights', can pull us down in battle, make us lose focus on the larger picture, and even cost us our very purpose. Just as the hunter was distracted from his main prize by the grasshopper, we, too, can be led astray by harbouring negativity.

In the battlefield of life, to truly succeed and claim victory, we must shed unnecessary weight. We must let go of the trivial distractions and focus on the bigger picture. For it's only when we release these burdens that we can truly soar to our destined heights.

And remember, sometimes, those causing you pain are mere grasshoppers, oblivious to the chaos they create. Don't let them divert you from your path. Stay focused, shed the weight, and march forward to your destiny.

Weights in the Wilderness

In the journey of life and faith, the concept of 'shedding weights' is instrumental in deepening our connection with the Lord. It is about releasing the burdens, both tangible and intangible, that hinder our spiritual progress and obstruct our path to true communion with God. By holding onto these weights, we unknowingly erect barriers that limit our spiritual growth and often lead to stagnation.

Understanding the Weights

The 'weights' can manifest in various forms in our lives. They could be emotional burdens like bitterness, resentment, or unforgiveness. They might also be physical or materialistic attachments that we cling to, such as certain lifestyles, habits, or even objects that we have given undue importance. Sometimes, they might be personal idols, things, or concepts that we've placed above God in our lives.

The Bible says in Hebrews 12:1: 'Therefore we also, since we are surrounded by so great a cloud of witnesses, let us lay aside every weight, and the sin which so easily ensnares us, and let us run with endurance the race that is set before us . . .'

This verse aptly captures the essence of shedding weights. It underscores the importance of relinquishing anything that impedes our spiritual race.

Consequences of Holding On to Weights

By holding on to these weights, we do more harm to ourselves than we realise. For one, they cause emotional and spiritual pain, acting as constant reminders of past hurt or present struggles.

They also cause a delay in our spiritual journey. The Holy Spirit seeks to guide, comfort, and empower us, but these weights can obstruct His work within us.

Ephesians 4:30-32 reminds us: 'And do not grieve the Holy Spirit of God, by whom you were sealed for the day of redemption. Let all bitterness, wrath, anger, clamour, and evil speaking be put away from you, with all malice. And be kind to one another, tenderhearted, forgiving one another, even as God in Christ forgave you.'

This verse emphasises that our negative emotions and actions can indeed grieve the Holy Spirit. It's a call to cleanse our hearts and spirits of these detrimental weights.

The Power of Letting Go

Letting go of these weights doesn't just free us from their burden, but it also paves the way for the Holy Spirit to work more profoundly within us. Without these barriers, we become more receptive to God's guidance, wisdom, and love.

Galatians 5:25 states: 'If we live in the Spirit, let us also walk in the Spirit.'

To keep in step with the Spirit, we must continually evaluate our lives, discern the weights that hold us back, and, with God's help, cast them aside. It's a process, often slow, as God moulds us and teaches us patience, waiting for us to relinquish these weights.

Letting Go of My Weights

One of the most challenging aspects of this wilderness journey is the process of identifying and then shedding the weights that hold us back from true fellowship with God. For me, the revelation of these weights came during one of the most challenging periods of my life: my battle with cancer.

Cancer is not just a battle of the body; it is a battle of the mind, soul, and spirit. It's a war waged on multiple fronts, and each front requires its own strategy, its own weapons. My initial understanding of shedding weights was superficial, limited to materialistic weights like makeup and shoes. I believed that by letting go of these superficial attachments, I was lightening my load for the spiritual journey ahead.

However, in the midst of my treatment, I made a profound discovery. The heaviest weight I carried was not material but emotional—bitterness. This bitterness was more toxic than the cancer I was fighting. It was a silent killer, slowly poisoning my spirit and obstructing my connection with God.

The Bible reminds us in Ephesians 4:31-32: 'Let all bitterness, wrath, anger, clamour, and evil speaking be put away from you, with all malice. And be kind to one another, tenderhearted, forgiving one another, even as God in Christ forgave you.'

Recognising the weight of bitterness was just the first step. The real challenge lay in shedding it. It took a month of soul-searching, praying, and confiding in my spiritual mentor. I had to confront my pain, the feeling of betrayal, and abandonment by my own family during my darkest hour. I had to grapple with these emotions, acknowledge them, and then decide to let them go.

The devil, as always, was keen to remind me of my pain, to keep the wounds fresh. But each time those memories surfaced, I turned to God in prayer. I reminded myself that perhaps God had allowed this abandonment so that I could draw closer to Him, to rely solely on His strength and not on human support. This perspective was inspired by Isaiah 42:8: 'I am the Lord, that is My name; And My glory I will not give to another, Nor My praise to carved images.'

By viewing my trials through this lens, I began to see them not as punishments, but as opportunities. Opportunities for growth, for deeper communion with God, and for a stronger, more resilient spirit.

In the end, the act of shedding these emotional weights was not just about lightening my load for the spiritual journey; it was about survival. By letting go of bitterness, I was not only drawing closer to God, but also giving myself a fighting chance against cancer. The battle with cancer was not just about defeating the disease in my body, but also about achieving victory over the emotional and spiritual weights that threatened to drag me down.

To anyone struggling with their emotional burdens, I urge you to identify them, confront them, and, with God's help, shed them. Your spiritual journey will be all the lighter and brighter for it.

Forgiveness: The Key to Unhindered Prayers

One of the most powerful lessons I learnt on my journey was the significance of forgiveness. It's a subject we often touch upon in religious contexts, but seldom do we internalise its true essence. The Lord's Prayer, which we recite so often, contains a profound truth: '. . . forgive us our trespasses, as we forgive those who trespass against us'. The weight of unforgiveness was one of the heaviest burdens I carried, and it was hindering my prayers.

Unforgiveness is a silent toxin. It brews in the corners of our hearts, often unnoticed, but its effects are potent. When we harbour bitterness and resentment, it's as if we are drinking poison and expecting the other person to die. The person whom you haven't forgiven might be living their life blissfully unaware, while you're the one bearing the weight of that unforgiveness.

Releasing this weight was liberating. It not only opened the heavens for my prayers, but also brought profound peace to my soul. When you genuinely forgive, it's like setting a prisoner free and then realising the prisoner was you.

Discovering True Beauty

During this transformative phase, I also came face-to-face with the societal standards of beauty. I, like many, was ensnared by the cosmetics, fashion, and the constant need to 'keep up'. But the more I looked inwards, the more I realised that true beauty wasn't about makeup or the latest fashion trends. True beauty is about embracing who God made you to be.

The Bible reminds us in Psalm 139:14, 'I praise you because I am fearfully and wonderfully made; your works are wonderful; I know that full well.' I began to see that when we clothe ourselves in Christ, we radiate a beauty that no cosmetic product can provide.

It's not about shunning material things or makeup. It's about understanding their place in our lives. When they take up a space reserved for God, it's a problem. The days I spent overindulging in materialistic pursuits were days I could have spent deepening my relationship with God.

The Song of the Soul

It was during this period of introspection and spiritual awakening that the song 'Give Me You' was birthed. It was a heart's cry, a desperate plea, an admission of my need for Christ. The world offers fleeting contentment, but in Christ, there is lasting joy, peace, and true beauty. In Him, there's no competition, no rat race. Just pure, unconditional love. Here are the lyrics:

Give me you, oh Lord, Give
me you, Holy Ghost, Give
me you, oh Lord, Give me
you.

Verse 1
Jehovah Nissi, My strong tower,
The Lily of the Valley, My hiding place.
Refuge from my storm, My sufficient God,
Give me You, Jesus, Emmanuel. Give me You, oh Lord,
Give me You, Holy Ghost, Give me You, oh Lord, Give me You.

Verse 2
My life without You is full of crises.
Riches without You, Jesus, equals poverty and wretchedness.
My beauty without You is all in vain.
My life without You is full of crises. When You are far
away from me, Jesus,
My life is messed up; my life is full of crises.

Give me You, Jesus,
Give me You, my strong tower. I need you, Jesus,
I make myself available to You, Lord. Holy Spirit, give me You.

Give me You, oh Lord,
Give me You, Holy Ghost, Give
me you, oh Lord, Give me You.

GIVE ME YOU by Chidimma D. Onohua

To anyone reading this, if you ever feel weighed down by societal standards or the shackles of unforgiveness, remember, in Christ, you are enough. You are beautiful, not because of what you wear or how you look, but because you are made in the image of God. Embrace that truth, let go of the weights, and walk in the freedom Christ offers.

Finding Strength in the Midst of Battle

Everyone encounters battles in their life. These battles, often more mental and spiritual than physical, can be gruelling and taxing. Yet, it's during these times that we learn the most about ourselves and our relationship with God.

When life seems overwhelming, and God appears silent, it's a test of faith. It's a reminder of 2 Corinthians 5:7: 'For we live by faith, not by sight.' The silence of God does not signify His absence. It is an invitation to lean in more deeply, to exercise our faith, and to shed the weights that hinder us.

However, in these silent times, it's essential to be aware of the devil's tactics. He will try to bring distractions, frustrations, bitterness, and anger into your life. Ephesians 6:11 tells us, 'Put on the full armour of God, so that you can take your stand against the devil's schemes.' The battle isn't just about facing external challenges, but managing the internal ones that could derail our faith and purpose.

It's crucial to understand that when you're in the midst of a fierce battle, it often signifies a change of season. Just as nature has its storms before the calm and rejuvenation, our lives follow a similar pattern. The fiercer the battle, the more significant the breakthrough that awaits. Just as Romans 8:28 reminds us, 'And we know that in all things God works for the good of those who love him, who have been called according to his purpose.'

The intensity of the challenges you face is directly proportional to the greatness that lies ahead. The enemy will always try to hinder your progress when he senses you're on the brink of a significant breakthrough. Thus, it's essential to guard your spirit, feed it with the Word of God, and ensure it's robust enough to withstand the attacks.

When the pain and the challenges increase, it's a sign that your breakthrough is near. Think of it like the labour pains a woman goes through before the birth of a child. The pain signifies something beautiful is about to emerge.

In conclusion, as you navigate the battles of life:

1. **Stay Rooted in Faith:** Even when God seems silent, trust in His plan and promises. Your faith will be your compass.

2. **Guard Your Spirit:** Be aware of the devil's tactics and put on the full armour of God.
3. **Anticipate a New Season:** Challenges often precede significant breakthroughs. Prepare yourself for the new that's coming.
4. **Focus on the Prize:** Don't get bogged down by the present pain. Keep your eyes on the purpose and the promise.
5. **Pray Continuously:** Prayer is your most potent weapon. Use it diligently.

As Galatians 6:9 says, 'And let us not grow weary while doing good, for in due season we shall reap if we do not lose heart.' Your season of harvest is coming. Stay the course, and remember that every battle is preparing you for a brighter, more blessed tomorrow.

AFFIRMATIONS:

1. I will unashamedly live for God, not man.
2. God covers me with His feathers; I find refuge under His wings.
3. God is intentional in my life; all things are working for my good.

CHAPTER 13

Dreams and Revelations

In my journey of faith, one of the most profound ways in which God brought light into the darkness of my life was through the avenue of divine dreams and revelations. It was through these remarkable experiences that I discovered a deeper connection with God, an intimate channel through which God chose to communicate with me (Acts 2:17; Genesis 20:3).

Why talk about dreams, you may wonder? Well, there are several compelling reasons dreams have played such a pivotal role in my spiritual life:

1. Did you know that we spend approximately one-third of our lives sleeping? It's a significant portion of our existence that is often overlooked. Within those hours of slumber lies a world of potential, where God can impart His wisdom and guidance to us, according to Job 33:14-16.

2. Another intriguing aspect of dreams is that everyone dreams. Even those who claim not to dream simply don't remember their dreams. It's a shared human experience that transcends cultural, linguistic, and geographic boundaries. This means God can speak to anyone through dreams.

3. **Dreams are biblical:** Dreams have a deep-rooted biblical significance. In the Book of Joel 2:28, it is written: 'And it shall come to pass afterward that I will pour out My Spirit on all flesh; your sons and your daughters shall prophesy, your old men shall dream dreams, your young men shall see visions.'

This verse from the Old Testament clearly affirms the divine nature of dreams and visions. It underscores that God uses dreams as a means to communicate His will and guidance to humanity. Furthermore, in the Book of Acts 2, we see the fulfilment of this prophecy, as the Holy Spirit descended upon the disciples, empowering them to proclaim the message of Christ.

Through my personal experiences, I have come to believe that dreams are something we should never ignore. These experiences have not only provided me with guidance but have also shown me that, even in the darkest of times, God's light can shine brightly through the medium of dreams.

Carrying the Family Burden

I had a dream where I was in a farmland, and an old man placed a heavy coffin on my head. This dream occurred over twenty years ago. I was in tears, standing in that field, asking, 'What do you want me to do with this burden on my head?' He replied, 'You're the only one who can carry it. That's your family. That's for you. That's your family's problem.'

I believe this dream signified I was destined to bear the burden of the spirit of death and to deliver my family from it. The coffin symbolises a weighty, unresolved family issue or the presence of the spirit of death. This dream reflected my calling to uplift my family and to pray against death's influence within my family. It suggests that I possess the grace, strength, and capability to confront and resolve family problems, even when they seem overwhelming.

Check Your Dreams

I remember vividly that I was at my brother's place at a certain time in Liverpool. I had gone to his parish in Liverpool when I had this dream. In the dream, everyone, including my parents, siblings, and others, were cursing me, saying things like, 'It will never be well with you.' I was deeply hurt, and tears streamed down my face in the dream. I pleaded with them, telling them I had sacrificed so much for them, and this was how they treated me.

This dream occurred in 2010–2011. When I woke up, it was around 5:30 a.m., and I found myself crying in real life. I immediately reached for my phone and called my dad, who was in Nigeria. I said, 'Daddy, did you curse me?' He was surprised and asked why I was calling so early. I explained what had happened in the dream and told him that everyone, including my siblings, had cursed me. I was in tears as I asked him what I had done to deserve it.

My dad assured me he had not cursed me, and he said my mom was also there. He assured me they were not behind any curse. I then asked him if he could bless me, and he agreed. Over the phone, my dad blessed me in the name of the Father, the Son, and the Holy Spirit, and he declared that he was breaking every curse. He reassured me that the devil was trying to deceive me and that he could never curse me. His blessing brought me comfort and peace.

After talking to my dad, I rushed to find the Reverend Father, whom I considered a father figure and confronted him about the dream. I asked him why he had cursed me. He prayed for me and blessed me.

The lesson here is clear: if anything transpires in a dream, do not accept it blindly without verification. Dreams, though powerful, can often be symbolic or misleading.

Furthermore, if negative events unfold in your dream life, it's essential to take action in your waking life to counteract them. Just like I did, I was cursed in the dream and was blessed when I woke up to counter that. Dreams can sometimes serve as spiritual or subconscious messages, and addressing their negative aspects can be a proactive way to shape your reality in a positive direction. So, always be attentive to the messages your dreams may carry and take steps to ensure your well-being and spiritual growth.

From Darkness to Healing

I had a dream concerning my youngest sister as a warning of a health challenge that was going to come upon her. In this dream, the three of us, my two sisters and I, found ourselves in a desolate and pitch-black wilderness. We were running in endless circles within this darkness, seemingly trapped for what felt like two decades. The place offered no escape or exit, and we were trapped in a seemingly never-ending cycle.

Then, one fateful day after those long twenty years, my youngest sister suddenly shouted in excitement, 'I see light! I see light coming from somewhere!' She had spotted a glimmer of hope—a path to follow. Her discovery spurred me and my other sister to follow her as she made her way toward the source of the light. She was determined, urging us to join her on this newfound path.

As we ventured further, we encountered a wide chasm that we needed to leap across to reach the light. My younger sister bravely took the first leap, calling back to encourage us, 'Come on, big sister, you can do it!' I was hesitant, considering the vastness of the gap, but eventually, I summoned the courage and jumped across to join her.

Now, it was just my younger sister left on the other side. We called out to her, urging her to take the leap and join us. We reminded her of the twenty long years we had spent in that dark wilderness and how it was finally time to go home. She acknowledged the light but unexpectedly turned her attention to a patch of vegetables she claimed to have seen. We were bewildered; how had she noticed such beautiful vegetables in the darkness?

Before we could persuade her to jump, she darted back into the wilderness, running towards the imagined vegetables. I had no choice but to jump back and pursue her, determined to bring her to safety. As I reached her, she insisted the vegetables were too beautiful to leave behind. I agreed, telling her I could see them too, and that they were indeed magnificent.

With great care, I lifted her onto my shoulders, her weight on my neck, and I jumped across the gap once more, carrying her to safety. We finally crossed over, and as we approached the light, I noticed a sign that read, 'Welcome to South Africa.' It was a symbol of the new beginning and hope that awaited us.

In the wake of my sister's struggles with her mental health, I couldn't help but recall this dream. My younger sister, the first to leap toward the light, reminded me of my pivotal role in her journey of healing. This dream was once again God bringing light into the dark desert. My sister was completely healed and delivered.

Revelation About Witches

In this dream, I found myself in my family's house, or perhaps it was a symbolic representation of a place deeply rooted in my family's history. The atmosphere was heavy, with rain pouring down relentlessly and the land ravaged by erosion, threatening the safety of the homes.

In this surreal journey, I had a mission to unlock something crucial for my family's well-being. I felt a sense of urgency, as if time itself was against me. It wasn't the first time that something led me back to my family's home. Sometimes, it felt like a powerful wind would transport me there when significant events were about to unfold.

Amid the tempestuous weather, I spotted an old, dilapidated car, a relic from a bygone era. Deserted and devoid of any human presence, it seemed incongruous in the midst of the raging storm. Undeterred, I climbed into the weathered vehicle and attempted to drive it despite the relentless floodwaters.

As I struggled to navigate the flooded terrain, the voices of onlookers from their windows filled the air. They warned me that the storm would surely be my undoing, that the flood would carry me away, but I pressed on. The water began to seep into the car, yet I remained steadfast in my determination.

I was on a mission to find the keys, and nothing would deter me. The villagers watched in disbelief, wondering how I could persevere against such adversity.

Finally, I reached a specific location, a house that held

significance from my childhood visits to the village: a mud house. Inside, I encountered a group of women, familiar faces from my past, some of whom were still alive in reality. They were engaged in a peculiar activity, pounding something with a rhythmic intensity. God revealed to me that these were witches!

As I observed them, I heard cries emanating from the depths of the mortar they were pounding. These were the voices of people, and many of them were the innocent voices of children. It was a disconcerting sight, and I watched in both horror and understanding.

One woman confronted me, questioning my audacity to be there. She accused me of being ignorant of their practices, but I stood my ground. I demanded the return of the keys, adamant that I would not allow them to continue their malevolent actions.

They challenged me to retrieve the keys, which they claimed were in the mortar. I approached cautiously, not willing to put my hands into that ominous mixture. An elderly man retrieved a bunch of keys from the mortar and handed them to me.

With the keys in my possession, I left the house, but not before one of the women called my attention to something—a hair comb that I had left behind. It was a cherished possession of mine, but I decided to leave it with them, sensing it might be a trap to reclaim the keys.

Upon waking, I was left with a sense of uncertainty about the purpose of this dream. It felt like a revelation, a glimpse into the presence of forces that needed to be reckoned with. It reminded me of God's protective hand over His children and how He unveils things to come in order to safeguard His own. In the Bible, this theme of divine revelation and protection is found in various verses, such as Isaiah 41:10: 'Fear not, for I am with you; be not dismayed, for I am your God. I will strengthen you, yes, I will help you, I will uphold you with My righteous right hand.'

This dream served as a reminder that God reveals things to protect His children, even in the face of adversity and the unknown.

The Dream That Foretold My Cancer Battle

I had another dream, and in this dream, God was warning me about my cancer diagnosis. It was a deeply unsettling experience, especially because my mother had succumbed to cancer, and she also appeared in the dream. In this night vision, I found myself on her bed, and she kept urging me to leave, pushing me away from it. I resisted, wanting to stay where she was, but she insisted I go. This repeated until I woke up. It was as if my mother was telling me to get checked, to go to the hospital, and not let her fate become mine.

The next day, after the dream, I felt a lump, and it sent shivers down my spine. A week later, I started noticing pores on my breast, and even worse, I saw blood coming out. I felt a wave of fear and despair wash over me, and I knew I had to find answers.

I began to research and educate myself about what could be happening. As I looked into my symptoms, I couldn't help but hope that it wasn't cancer. I prayed to God fervently, pleading for this nightmare to pass me by. However, all the signs pointed to the dreadful possibility, and I couldn't shake off my fear and anger. I felt a sense of frustration, questioning why I had to endure such pain and uncertainty.

In my desperation, I resisted going to the hospital. I couldn't bear the thought of facing a cancer diagnosis, and I was exhausted from the endless hospital visits. I just wanted it all to end, one way or another. So, I ignored a referral for an ultrasound for two months, allowing my anger and despair to consume me.

Despite initially ignoring her message, I eventually mustered the courage to listen. I prayed and sought guidance, and it became clear that I needed to face whatever lay ahead. When I finally went to the hospital, the diagnosis confirmed my worst fear—cancer.

Looking back, I realise that this dream was a divine warning, a premonition of my cancer diagnosis. God used the image of my mother to push me towards getting medical help, just as she would have wanted. It was a painful and frightening journey, but I believe that God's intervention and my mother's guidance in that dream ultimately saved my life.

Work Colleague Dream

I had a dream about a colleague of mine who used to cover for me whenever I was unavailable. It seemed like she had always been drawn to my job, preferring it over her own for some inexplicable reason. In the dream, I saw her writing my name on a white piece of paper and then covering it with blood. She then took this paper to one of my bosses' offices.

The following day, when I arrived at the office, I couldn't help but give her a suspicious look. It was as though I could sense that something was amiss, even before any developments occurred. I had been praying about this since the dream, and although there have been moments of fear, my prayer partners have reassured me that whoever sent this negative influence is attempting to take my position.

Nonetheless, I believe that if she indeed did something

negative, it was allowed by God for a purpose, and it has led me to where I am today.

Health Issue Revealed

I had another intriguing dream involving my colleague, whom I used to work with back in 2007 or 2008. We were both contract staff for Chevron at the time. My colleague was a brilliant and sharp engineer, and in this particular dream, I saw him receiving a new Chevron ID card, but it was not the usual green ID for contract staff; it was a blue ID meant for regular Chevron employees.

The next morning at the office, I couldn't help but share this dream with him. I told him, 'Hey, bro, I had a dream about you. I think Chevron is going to convert your contract into a permanent position soon.' He chuckled and dismissed my prediction, saying he was actually planning to resign in the following week. He had received a job offer from another oil company, offering a contract position with higher pay than Chevron.

I pleaded with him, 'Please, reconsider. Don't accept that offer just yet. I truly believe that Chevron is going to convert you.' I insisted he pray about it and make his decision based on what he felt led to do. Ultimately, he didn't resign.

Two months later, to my delight and his amazement, my

colleague received a conversion offer from Chevron and became a permanent employee. He often tells the story of how I had foreseen this in a dream, and he now advises people to take dreams seriously if someone like me has had a dream about them.

Fast forward to 2023, in late March, I dreamt of him once again. This time, he approached me with a look of sadness on his face. He confessed he wasn't feeling well, and when I asked if he was sick, he replied, 'Yes, my heart is failing, and the doctors say I'm not going to live much longer.' In the dream, I held him close, prayed fervently for about five minutes, and even spoke in tongues.

When I woke up, I felt compelled to reach out to him. I had learnt not to keep such dreams to myself. I messaged him, asking if he was okay. He replied that he was fine. I then shared the details of the dream with him. I reassured him that whatever had been seen in the dream had been reversed and taken care of by God. Later, he confirmed that he had some health challenges. In April, he and his wife visited me in the UK while they were there for medical check-ups. They brought me gifts from Nigeria, and I was relieved to see that he was indeed fine, just as I had believed and prayed for.

Healing of My Younger Brother

I remember a dream I had back in 2022, shortly after being discharged from LUTH hospital. In the dream, I saw my younger brother. We were at a wedding, and someone pointed him out to me. I couldn't believe it was him because he appeared extremely ill in the dream. I questioned if he was indeed my brother, but he confirmed it, and I asked why he looked so skinny.

In the dream, he said he was dying, and I held him in that room as he pleaded for help. Then I woke up. It had been six months since I was discharged from LUTH in Nigeria due to DVT (deep vein thrombosis), which had made flying inadvisable.

In January 2022, I left Nigeria against my doctor's advice to come to the UK. Before leaving Nigeria, I had obtained some local herbs from a market. When I arrived at my brother's house in Bristol, he was in poor condition and couldn't speak. I immediately went to the kitchen, prepared the herbs, and gave them to him to drink.

The next day, he called our dad, saying he was well again and couldn't explain how it had happened. My dad often humorously referred to me as 'mom' because of my nurturing nature.

I spent about six months with my brother, even when he

contracted COVID. His case was severe, affecting his lungs and causing infections. He was passing out, and I was there with him, despite also contracting COVID. Everyone was concerned for my health due to my existing condition, but I was the one taking care of him. I remember one night when his condition worsened and he was passing out. I held him and prayed with him for hours, and eventually, he recovered.

The decision to make that trip to the UK was influenced by the dream I had. God reveals to redeem.

The Healing of My Sister

In another dream in 2012, I saw my elder sister; she was very sick, and she was dying. I was offshore at the time. At this time, I hadn't spoken with my sister in a long time. I think we had this misunderstanding, and we didn't talk to each other for five years. So when I had this dream, I saw her, and it was as if life was leaving her.

She stretched out her hands and said, 'Chidimma, help me, help me to live.' I could see her dying, so I stretched out my hands and pulled her out. I woke up at about 2 a.m. After praying, I sent her a message. Remember, we hadn't spoken in five years? So, you know, the devil would say, 'She left you; she stopped talking to you. So what do you want?' But the Holy Spirit was saying, 'Hey, you need to speak to your sister.' So I picked up my phone and sent her a message. I said, 'I hope you're okay. I had a dream. Are you alright? Please talk to me.' And I was so shocked that immediately after I sent that message, it wasn't even two minutes before she responded. She said, 'Chidimma, I am sick; I am scheduled for surgery on my womb. I want to get my womb removed, and I'm scared. I'm very sick.' And I said, in the name of Jesus Christ, 'I reverse that womb condition! They're not taking your womb out. You are healed in Jesus's name.'

I left offshore about three days later, and when I got home the next day, I drove straight to Canaan Land. That's where I used to have my quiet time with God, at Winners Chapel. I checked into one of the compound houses and stayed there for about five days. Every day, I would go to the altar, kneel, write my sister's name, and place it at the altar. I prayed fervently. I was there for about five days. On the fifth day, it was a Sunday. After the service, I went to the altar again. I wrote her name and placed it on the altar, leaving it there under the carpet.

My sister called me the next week to say, 'We went to the hospital, and the surgery has been cancelled. I'm fine; there's nothing wrong with me anymore.' That was a miracle. We started talking again, and she eventually came back to Nigeria the following year, in 2013. When she came, I took her to my church, and she shared the testimony detailing how God had saved her life through her sister.

Juju Priest Exposed

In the offshore company where I used to work, I had a colleague who everyone called JP, which stood for 'Juju Priest.' The term 'Juju Priest' is often associated with individuals who practise voodoo. He and I worked in the same department, and it was well-known that he had a shrine dedicated to certain deities. Surprisingly, despite his mysterious aura, he had numerous wives, including several affluent women. I often wondered how he managed to charm so many women, suspecting his voodoo practices played a role.

One vivid night, I had an unsettling dream. I found myself standing on barren land, completely exposed in his shrine. JP was also about to get his clothes off. He began to say, 'Doris, come to me'. As I came close to him, a powerful voice said, 'Do not shake his hand again'. I believe this to be the voice of God. This advice was so forceful that I woke up remembering it distinctly.

The next day, as I headed to my office, I encountered JP. The first thing he said was, 'Doris, shake my hand.' Instantly, I recalled the warning from my dream. Though I used to casually greet him with a handshake, I declined this time, citing my dream as the reason. He seemed taken aback.

Later, a colleague approached me. He was curious about my dream, so I recounted it to him. His reaction was startling. He said that just the previous day, JP had confided in him, expressing a determined intent to 'get' me, regardless of the cost. He had brushed it off initially, thinking of me as someone JP couldn't easily influence. But after hearing about my dream, he was genuinely concerned.

The revelation left me overwhelmed, and I broke down in tears. My colleague, in his shock, commented that there was something extraordinary about me, wondering if I was more than just a regular human.

AFFIRMATIONS:

1. I can overcome everything with Christ.
2. I'm a temple of the Holy Spirit.
3. I'm united with the Lord and one spirit with Him.

Chapter 14

Being a Vessel

From a tender age, there was an inkling deep within me, an unshakeable feeling that I was destined for something unique. I sensed a higher calling, a pull towards a purpose beyond the ordinary. As I grew, this feeling intensified, and by the time I was sixteen, I found myself seeking spiritual guidance. I went from church to church, meeting with various men of God, from Catholic reverend fathers to Pentecostal pastors, hoping to find clarity, hoping to receive a touch that would set everything into place.

Yet, despite the many prayers, prophecies, and deliverance

sessions, the void within me persisted. It was as if a puzzle piece was missing from my soul's jigsaw, and no matter how hard I searched, it eluded me. But then came the realisation, the moment of profound insight. The divine wasn't seeking to send me a messenger or guide me through another. Instead, God wanted *me*. He yearned for my time, my devotion, my complete surrender. It became clear that until I genuinely answered this divine call, nothing would fall into place.

Over the years, trusted pastors and revered spiritual leaders had told me the same thing: 'God wants you. Stop running from Him.' Yet, I'd been in denial, thinking that there was another way, thinking that the prophecies and prayers alone would set everything right. But when they didn't come to pass, doubt crept in. I began to question these spiritual leaders, even deeming some as untruthful. Why did their prophecies change lives for others, but not for me? Why did their prayers create miracles for some but leave me in the same spot?

The answer was simple, yet profound. The Lord was revealing things to me, not for me to passively wait, but for me to take action. Each dream, each vision, was a call to step up, to be the vessel through which His will would manifest. It was a reminder that sometimes, God doesn't send us to prophets or pastors;

sometimes, He calls us to be one.

And so, to anyone reading this, if you find yourself in a similar place, remember that sometimes the answer isn't outside but within. Sometimes, God isn't calling you to seek, but to be sought. Sometimes, He's not asking you to listen to another's voice but to find and trust your own, for in it lies His message for you.

The Story of Jeremiah

Jeremiah, often referred to as the 'weeping prophet', is one of the most prominent figures in the Old Testament. His story, as detailed in the Book of Jeremiah, is one of unwavering faith, deep anguish, and prophetic clarity.

From the outset, Jeremiah's calling was profound. In Jeremiah 1:5, the Lord says to him, 'Before I formed you in the womb I knew you, before you were born I set you apart; I appointed you as a prophet to the nations.' This declaration not only establishes Jeremiah's purpose but also underlines the divine orchestration of his life even before his birth. God had chosen him as a vessel, as a mouthpiece, to convey His messages to the people of Judah.

However, Jeremiah's initial response to this divine call was one of hesitancy and self-doubt. He replied, 'Ah, Sovereign Lord, I do not know how to speak; I am only a child' (Jeremiah 1:6). This reaction is relatable to many who feel inadequate or unprepared when faced with a significant task or calling. But God reassured Jeremiah, telling him not to be afraid and promising His unceasing support and presence.

As Jeremiah began to embrace his role, he faced immense challenges. His prophecies, which often warned of impending doom and called for repentance, were not well-received. He was persecuted, mocked, and even imprisoned. Yet, throughout these trials, Jeremiah remained a vessel for God's Word, delivering messages with unflinching honesty.

Jeremiah's life serves as a powerful testament to the idea of being a vessel for the Lord. From a young age, he was set apart, and even though he faced countless adversities, his dedication to his prophetic calling never wavered. Like the narrative in the previous chapter, Jeremiah's story underscores the concept that sometimes God doesn't call the equipped; He equips the called. Being a vessel means understanding and embracing this divine orchestration, even when the path seems challenging or unclear.

God's Jealousy: The Fiery Pursuit of His Chosen Vessels

When we traverse the realm of the divine and discuss the characteristics attributed to God, one facet that often raises eyebrows and stirs the pot of theological debate is His jealousy. The notion of a jealous God can be difficult to reconcile with the image of an all-loving, benevolent deity. So, what does this divine jealousy signify?

In Exodus 34:14, we are confronted with the declaration: 'For you shall worship no other god, for the Lord, whose name is Jealous, is a jealous God.' At a cursory glance, this can feel disconcerting. Why would the Creator of the universe, who holds everything in His hands, exhibit an emotion we so commonly associate with human insecurity?

It's crucial to understand that God's jealousy isn't akin to human jealousy. It doesn't stem from insecurity or pettiness. Instead, it originates from a place of righteous love and fierce protectiveness. God's jealousy is His zealous commitment to what's best for us, His creation. It's a holy longing to keep us from harm's way, especially the harm we unknowingly inflict upon ourselves when we stray from His path.

Some question, 'Why would God go to great lengths, sometimes even allowing afflictions, to get our undivided attention?' Well, like a masterful artist passionately protective of their magnum opus, God's fervour for us is unparalleled. Especially when He has a divine assignment for us, He will take measures to ensure we are aligned with His purpose.

Consider Job, for instance. Here was a man of impeccable righteousness, and yet God allowed Satan to test his faith by stripping away all he held dear. Some might say, 'How could a loving God permit such suffering?' But the narrative of Job is less about suffering and more about unwavering faith amidst adversity. God knew Job's heart. He trusted Job to remain steadfast. And in the end, Job's losses were restored manifold, showcasing God's redeeming love.

In understanding God's jealousy, it's vital to grasp that His ways are higher than our ways. His love for us is so profound that He desires nothing less than our whole heart. When we divert our worship, our love, our obsession towards other 'gods'—be they material possessions, relationships, or ambitions—we inadvertently place barriers between us and the fullness of God's love.

So, rather than viewing God's jealousy as a flaw or a sign of vindictiveness, let's see it for what it truly is: a testament to His unyielding love for us. It's an invitation to draw closer, to lean in, and to experience the depth of His passion for each one of us. In this light, God's jealousy is not a threat but a promise—a promise that He will always pursue us, no matter how far we stray.

Where Did These Troubles Come From?

From the many questions and reflections that have arisen in my journey, one stands out prominently: the origin of my cancer. When I was diagnosed, a whirlwind of emotions consumed me, and many around me questioned its source. 'Did it come from God?' they'd ask, some with genuine concern, others with veiled accusations.

I want to set the record straight: my cancer did not come from God.

The Bible is clear about the nature of our Heavenly Father. He is a God of love, mercy, and healing. He is not the author of pain, suffering, or disease. Instead, it's the enemy, the devil, who comes to steal, kill, and destroy. It's essential to understand this distinction, especially when grappling with life's trials and tribulations.

Many times, in our limited understanding, we associate our pain and challenges directly with God's will. We wonder if He's punishing us or testing us. But the truth I've come to understand is that while God allows certain events in our lives, it doesn't mean He authors them.

In my case, the devil sought to break me with this affliction, to shatter my faith and deter me from my divine path. But God, in His infinite wisdom and love, used even this painful chapter to draw me closer to Him, to refine my faith, and to showcase His healing and redemptive power.

After enduring the arduous journey of major surgeries, including an appendectomy, fibroid removal, Bartholin's cyst treatment, laparotomy and bowel resection, and mastectomy due to cancer, I can declare that the righteous face many afflictions, yet God has delivered me from each one. His unwavering faithfulness has been a guiding light. When people ask me about my sickness, I tell them about the God I've come to know even better through this journey – a God who heals, restores, and redeems. A God whose love is so profound He brings *'Light Through The Dark Desert'*. He can turn them into opportunities for grace, growth, and testimony.

God's Permission and the Mystery of Suffering

One question that I am asked, especially during my trials and tribulations, and more so when I was diagnosed with cancer, is whether God allowed these challenges. This contemplation becomes even deeper when I think of God's nature, which I've always believed to be loving, caring, and protective.

Colossians 3:3 has been a guiding scripture for me. It speaks of the concept of dying to oneself and living for Christ. 'For you died, and your life is now hidden with Christ in God.' This passage has always signified a spiritual truth for me: when I give my life to Christ, my old self, with its worries and fears, dies, and my new self, embedded in Christ, comes alive.

So, the pressing question: *If the cancer didn't originate from God, did He permit it?*

From all I've learnt and experienced, God isn't the author of pain, sickness, or death. John 10:10 makes this clear, stating that the thief (the devil) has only one agenda: to steal, kill, and destroy. But Jesus, in stark contrast, came so we might have life and have it abundantly. While the cancer's origin wasn't God, I've come to understand that in His divine wisdom, He might permit certain trials for reasons that might escape our immediate understanding.

Why would a God, who I believe loves me deeply, allow such trials? It's a question I've pondered upon. Sometimes, it might be to refine and strengthen my faith, to pull me closer to Him, or to serve a purpose that is beyond my comprehension, but aligns with

His divine plan.

Looking back at my journey, I've had a profound revelation. While I seemed to be thriving on the outside, there was a deep internal struggle. This is where I've felt God's intense love, often described as jealousy. He yearns for our full attention, for us to wholly rely on Him. He never intended for me to suffer, but perhaps He wanted to draw me into a deeper, more intimate relationship with Him.

In permitting the cancer, I don't believe God was punishing me. Instead, I feel He might have been redirecting me, nudging me closer, and setting me on a path that aligns more closely with His purpose for my life. In this vulnerable state, my dependence on God became paramount. I truly realised that for anyone to reach or harm me, they'd first have to go through Christ and God the Father.

To conclude, from my perspective, God's permission isn't an act of cruelty; it's an act of love. Through my trials, I believe He's shaping me, moulding me, and drawing out the best in me, even from the furnace of affliction.

Embracing the Call to Be a Vessel

The journey of being a vessel is undeniably challenging, yet it's also deeply rewarding. Throughout this chapter, the intertwining of personal stories with biblical teachings paints a vivid picture of the relentless love and pursuit of God. Just as a potter meticulously shapes clay into a vessel, God, too, moulds us, refining and perfecting us for His purpose. The challenges, the trials, and even moments of doubt are all part of this divine sculpting process.

However, it's essential to remember that our relationship with the Divine isn't a passive one. While God's love is unwavering, our commitment, surrender, and action are paramount. It's a mutual dance, with God leading and us following, yet with every step, He desires our full engagement and passion.

For those called to be vessels, this is not just a journey of faith, but also one of action. Every revelation, every prompting, and every divine whisper is a call to move, to respond, and to align ourselves more deeply with God's will.

Action Steps for Those Called to Be Vessels:

1. **Self-Reflection:** Dedicate time regularly to introspect and discern where you are on your spiritual journey. Recognise

areas where you might resist God's call and seek guidance on how to yield more fully.

2. **Commit to Continuous Learning:** Engage in regular scriptural study, attend spiritual retreats, or join faith-based groups. The more you immerse yourself in spiritual teachings, the clearer God's call will become.
3. **Pray for Guidance:** Establish a consistent prayer routine. Seek clarity, strength, and wisdom in your role as a vessel.
4. **Seek Mentorship:** Identify spiritual leaders or mentors who can guide you, offer wisdom, and provide accountability.
5. **Share Your Testimony:** As you experience God's work in your life, share your stories with others. Your testimony can inspire and uplift many, guiding them toward their path as vessels.

In embracing these steps, remember that being a vessel is not just about being used by God, but also about experiencing the profound love, peace, and purpose He offers. As you walk this path, know that you are never alone, and every step, even the challenging ones, is a move closer to your divine destiny.

Below is the theme song for this book, which speaks of God's promise to elevate and make you a light. May this song minister to you.

Being a Vessel

Verse 1

I'm a pattern breaker. And a line crosser

A candidate of overflow My light has come.

And my light shines in darkness And darkness comprehends it not

I'm a shining light, even in dark desert. I illuminate my path

I illuminate my world

I illuminate everywhere I illuminate my path

I illuminate my world

I illuminate everywhere

Cos my light shines in darkness And darkness comprehends it not

I'm a bright shining light, even in dark desert.

Chorus

Light, through the dark desert Light, through the dark desert

I'm a shining light, even in dark desert. I'm a shining light, even in dark desert.

Verse 2

From the moment I was born He declared me a chosen race

A royal priesthood

Among the holy nation

A people for God's own possession He set me apart.

I'm a bright shining light, even in dark desert. I say, from the moment we were formed

He declared us a chosen race A royal priesthood

A holy nation

A people for Him

LIGHT THROUGH THE DARK DESERT by Chidimma D. Onuoha

You Are Unkillable

He set us apart, as the shining light We are shining,
we are shining Even in dark desert

Chorus
Light, through the dark desert Light, through the dark desert
I'm a shining light, even in dark desert. I'm a shining light,
even in dark desert.

Verse 3
Lift up your head, oh ye gates
Lift up your head, oh ye gates Be ye lifted, everlasting door
Be ye lifted, everlasting door And let me come in
I carry light I carry fire
I carry anointing
Ain't no stopping me – I shine No more delays – I shine
No more stagnation – I shine No more pain – I shine
No more limitation – I shine No more darkness – I shine I shine – I shine
I shine – I shine
Even in darkness – I shine I shine – I shine
I shine – I shine
In the day – I shine In the night – I shine

Chorus
Light, through the dark desert Light, through the dark desert
I'm a shining light, even in dark desert. I'm a shining light, even
in dark desert.

Being a Vessel

AFFIRMATIONS:

1. I'm a pattern breaker.
2. I'm a candidate for overflow.
3. I'm a shining light, even in dark deserts.

ABOUT THE AUTHOR

Chidimma Doris Onuoha is an individual whose life journey has been marked by resilience, perseverance, and multifaceted accomplishments. Having triumphed over ten major surgeries, including those for fibroid removal, appendectomy, Bartholin's cyst treatment, laparotomy and bowel resection, and mastectomy due to cancer, Chidimma has emerged as a beacon of strength and inspiration.

Professionally, Chidimma has held various pivotal roles, showcasing a diverse skill set. With a background as a Project Cost Engineer, Administrator, Business Analyst, Document Controller, and Life Coach, Chidimma has continually demonstrated adaptability and proficiency across multiple domains.

Chidimma's career trajectory includes significant stints at Chevron Nigeria Limited, where she excelled as an Office Administrator, Document Controller, Business/Cost Analyst, and finally as a highly acclaimed Project Cost Engineer from 2017 to 2023.

Beyond professional milestones, Chidimma's life has been peppered with noteworthy achievements. As a child, she garnered recognition for her portrayal of Adolphus Hitler in the drama *The Trial of Adolph Hitler*, earning the title of the most intelligent kid in school. An accomplished Gospel Singer and Minister, Chidimma released her debut album, *SUFFICIENT GRACE*, in 2002 and composed the revered Diversity Anthem, 'Diversity, the Chevron way,' for Chevron Nigeria Limited, receiving accolades for her contributions.

In 2017, Chidimma showcased her talent and artistry, securing the first runner-up position at Chevron's talent event with her rendition of Brenda Fassie's 'Vulindlela.' Her prowess as a Project Cost Controller has been acknowledged through numerous awards for excellence.

Outside her professional pursuits, Chidimma finds solace and passion in singing, travelling, and coaching. Her debut book marks a new chapter as a first-time author, reflecting her profound experiences and indomitable spirit.

Chidimma's life story is a testament to healing, light through the darkness, and determination. Her journey inspires others to overcome challenges and pursue their dreams against all odds.

About the Author

Two days after her last cancer treatment, she unveiled her foundation (Broad Shoulders Tribe).

BROAD SHOULDERS is a human development and community intervention tribe—a network of social innovators with the mandate to enable total wellness for a brighter life. With core strategic business/social functions in social research and training, manufacturing and production of organic sanitary wares, and building of sustainable health solutions, technology, and media integration for advocacy and policy formulation towards progressive medicine and charity for human advancement.

www.ingramcontent.com/pod-product-compliance
Lightning Source LLC
Chambersburg PA
CBHW020402080526
44584CB00014B/1132